More Praise for *The Art of Doing Good*

"Charles Bronfman and Jeff Solomon have followed upon their first collaboration with another thoughtful articulation of the tried-and-true rules of successful social entrepreneurship. At once accessible and engaging, *The Art of Doing Good* is a font of well-reasoned counsel for aspiring nonprofiteers."

—Adam Meyerson, president, Philanthropy Roundtable

"I knew from the beginning that I was going to enjoy and gain great information from *The Art of Doing Good*, and I looked forward to the content as I read from page to page. In this book I found affirmation and confirmation of what it takes to bring good ideas to full potential and to realize full value and sustainability that benefits, respects, and improves the quality of life for whoever will be affected. This book is a treasure trove for all of us who are eager to give back in meaningful and sustainable ways. Both the ideas and the people who have created them add to the joy of 'doing good' and are enriching my life. Thank you, Charles and Jeff!"

—Roselyne Chroman Swig, community activist

This work is lovingly dedicated to the memory of

Andrea Morrison Bronfman

*who refused to accept the status quo in any
philanthropic endeavor and urged all of us in that field
to enhance the future through innovation and risk taking.*

The Art *of* Doing Good

WHERE PASSION MEETS ACTION

Charles Bronfman

Jeffrey Solomon

with John Sedgwick

JOSSEY-BASS
A Wiley Imprint
www.josseybass.com

Author photo: Bill Stanton
Jacket design: Adrian Morgan

Published by Jossey-Bass
A Wiley Imprint
One Montgomery Street, Suite 1200, San Francisco, CA 94104-4594—www.josseybass.com

Jossey-Bass books and products are available through most bookstores. To contact Jossey-Bass directly call our Customer Care Department within the U.S. at 800-956-7739, outside the U.S. at 317-572-3986, or fax 317-572-4002.

Wiley publishes in a variety of print and electronic formats and by print-on-demand. Some material included with standard print versions of this book may not be included in e-books or in print-on-demand. If this book refers to media such as a CD or DVD that is not included in the version you purchased, you may download this material at http://booksupport.wiley.com. For more information about Wiley products, visit www.wiley.com.

Library of Congress Cataloging-in-Publication Data
Bronfman, Charles, 1931- author.
  The art of doing good : where passion meets action / Charles Bronfman and Jeffrey Solomon with John Sedgwick— First edition.
    pages cm
  Includes index.
   ISBN 978-1-118-26435-5 (hardback)
   ISBN 978-1-118-28574-9 (ebk.)
   ISBN 978-1-118-28246-5 (ebk.)
   ISBN 978-1-118-28464-3 (ebk.)
   1. Charities. 2. Nonprofit organizations—Management. I. Solomon, Jeffrey, author. II. Title.
  HV40.B866 2012
  361.7′630681—dc23
                                                        2012020106

Printed in the United States of America
FIRST EDITION
HB Printing   10 9 8 7 6 5 4 3 2 1

CONTENTS

v

PART THREE **Managing the Organization**

PART FOUR **Resources**

⸺⟶

PREFACE

WE HAVE TITLED THIS BOOK *The Art of Doing Good*. Now there's a concept. How exactly does one *do* good? It is much easier to imagine *being* good. But who is even to say what good is, let alone how to bring it about? After all, one person's good can be another person's bad—as evidenced by wars, political strife, and divorce. And, of course, *doing* good goes further, imposing one person's judgment about goodness on the world. That makes doing good suddenly seem rather . . . presumptuous, for how can anyone be so sure of what good is?

The *art* of doing good is not in recognizing and attempting to fill an unmet need but in taking the large view by carefully considering *all* the consequences of the effort to do good—both positive and negative.

In general, we consider it good to alleviate suffering and to promote satisfaction in this life. We put great stock in the psychologist Abraham Maslow's famous hierarchy of needs, which moves from food and shelter up to spiritual satisfaction. We believe it is always good to help people move up that hierarchy to ever greater fulfillment.

Still, it is probably because the good is complex, open to debate, and hard to certify when you get down to individual cases that those who try to do good are often derided as do-gooders. To us, there are few greater callings. In this book, we will use the term do-gooders occasionally to describe the social entrepreneurs we have selected to illustrate the themes of this book. We mean it as a compliment. For all our social leaders are bent on doing good in a mindful way. That is, they are aware of their own biases; conscious of the social, environmental, and financial implications of their efforts; respectful of cultural context; appropriately cautious about their abilities; and aware of the competition. But they also have a quality that is possibly more valuable than such an awareness, which is a willingness, if not an eagerness, to go for it and take a chance on change because they cannot bear to leave the world the way it is.

A word on terminology. We are inclined to refer to those featured in this book as social entrepreneurs, but we do so with a caution: strictly speaking, social entrepreneurs can be found on both sides of the for-profit and nonprofit divide, and are united in their belief in common entrepreneurial principles like finding new markets and applying strict measures of success. Social entrepreneurs are as likely to found a profit-minded philanthropy like Newman's Own as to start any of the ventures in this book. Nevertheless, because this book concentrates on nonprofits—being far more numerous and, we believe, far more potent entities for social change—our social entrepreneurs are drawn only from those ranks. We don't mean to suggest that there aren't other varieties of social entrepreneurs than the one we are describing here. It's just that there is no better word for the eighteen profiled in these pages. The terms *philanthropist, volunteer,* and *donor* don't come close to encapsulating their spirit, ambition, and ingenuity.

In their work, all these social entrepreneurs are guided by one overriding cause: helping others. This, after all, is the active element of the definition of philanthropy, which comes from the Greek for a love for mankind, and was first applied to Prometheus, who suffered to give men fire. But there is the irony. To help other people is selfless, but, as more than one social advocate has observed, it is selfish too—selfish in that the whole activity brings so much joy. For-profit enterprises are sustained by the profits they generate, but nonprofits live far more on good feelings, the joy of their results, which are possibly more rewarding than money.

This is the art of doing good.

The Art *of* Doing Good

"I'm looking for someone to do my part to make this a better world."

How to Change the World

THIS BOOK HAS A FAIRLY AUDACIOUS GOAL: to teach you how to change the world. Not through warfare, politics, or technology, but through a unique social invention, the nonprofit, that is intended to do good on a grand scale. The possibilities of nonprofits—or more formally not-for-profits—are limitless. They can knit communities together, protect refugees, promote world peace, transform education, preserve the environment, and salvage inner-city neighborhoods. You will read about all these endeavors here, along with eighteen remarkable men and women who've made them happen. We hope you can follow their example and our precepts to do similar things with nonprofits of your own. This is our book, of course, but it is also theirs, the eighteen, for they have contributed their wisdom on every page.

We are fans of nonprofits. We believe in their unique power to do good. Not just any nonprofit, though; only those that produce genuine innovations akin to the radical inventions on the for-profit side, like Facebook and the iPod. And, we should add, akin to the Jewish Federation, United Way, and Red Cross of a century ago, all of which caught on because they were daring for their day. In any case, no me-too entries need apply. Each must add its own unique contribution to the field. We like disruptive philanthropy—the kind that breaks eggs to make omelets.

Encouragement is needed, for this work is hard. Invariably, the mission is challenging, because, by definition, it has never before been attempted. The operational structure can be complex, and fraught with the tensions of any start-up. The financing is uncertain and sometimes nonexistent. The hours can be endless, the commitment total. Have we left anything out? It is not for everyone. But if the work is done wisely and well, and it bears fruit, the world will be much better for it, and so will you.

Philanthropy with No Money Down

Nonprofits are profoundly democratic entities, open to all, on the provider or recipient side, regardless of political affiliation. All that is required to start one is initiative. Yes, the airy notion of philanthropy often brings to mind the pet causes of the moneyed class or the charitable whims of image-buffing celebrities. But that's not true of all nonprofits, and it's certainly not true of the eighteen founders we have chosen to highlight here, nor of the people we'd like to attract to the cause.

Our previous book, *The Art of Giving: Where the Soul Meets a Business Plan,* was for and about donors. Though it dealt primarily with financial donations, it also laid out a broad philosophy of philanthropy that underpins this new volume. That philosophy has three parts:

1. As a philanthropic activist, you have to act with intentionality, with a purpose that brings forth your best effort. By the same

token, you should not feel guilt about any satisfaction you may take in your work. It's right and necessary. Without that satisfaction, the hard parts would just seem too hard.

2. Goals are essential, because you need to know what you are in this to accomplish.

3. It is never just you. You will collect a wide group of collaborators in this effort, and you will need them all.

Just three elements, you ask? Yes, basic ones, in the sense that three primary colors come together to make light. Philanthropy is about many things, but at bottom, every successful philanthropic effort requires drive, purpose, and connection. If you have these three, you are good to go.

Obviously, in order to give, one first has to have something to donate. So *The Art of Giving* is for readers with some discretionary income—as well as vision and industry. It is aimed at financial philanthropists, people who can change the world with their money and are searching for ways to derive measurement and meaning from their financial gifts. This new book is intended for those we would call active philanthropists, people who seek to change the world with their effort more than with their money. Whether they come from money or not, both types of philanthropists take pleasure in seeing their dreams realized in measurable ways. It is their version of a capitalist's return on investment. This kind of active philanthropy is open to anyone with a great idea about how to improve the world and a burning desire to make it happen. Open to you, say.

Before we go any further, though, we should introduce the eighteen visionaries whose insight and experience run through the book and give it the heft it has. It is not our book, really, but theirs. We have participated in start-ups and know the field, but they are the ones who have gone out there and done it—and then graciously reported back to us on what they have learned from their endeavors. This book would not exist without them.

The Eighteen

Solar Cooker Project
Rachel Andres, Founder and Director
www.jewishworldwatch.org/projects/ontheground/sudan
/solar-cooker-project

Operating under the auspices of Jewish World Watch, the Solar Cooker Project is designed to keep Darfuri women and girls safely in the refugee camps in Chad, free from the risk of rape and other forms of violence that might come from foraging for firewood for cooking.

───∽───

City Year, Inc.
Michael Brown, Chief Executive Officer and Cofounder
www.cityyear.org

City Year is an urban American Peace Corps. It deploys young people for a year of full-time, school-based community service to bolster educational resources and build democracy in America's cities through citizen service, civic leadership, and social entrepreneurship. City Year addresses the national dropout crisis by enlisting corps members to serve as tutors, mentors, and role models to help students stay in school or return to it.

───∽───

Harlem Children's Zone
Geoffrey Canada, President and Chief Executive Officer
www.hcz.org

The Harlem Children's Zone (HCZ) is a community-based organization serving more than seventeen thousand at-risk children; it takes a new holistic approach to ending the cycle of generational poverty in Harlem. Whereas other programs generally rely on institutions that, in turn, focus on school-age children, the HCZ invests in children from birth and enlists a village of adults to attain the critical mass necessary to keep them on the right educational path all the way through college and into the working world.

—∞—

STRIVE
Robert Carmona, Founder
www.strivenational.org

STRIVE aims right at the problem of chronic unemployment by encouraging idle workers to make major adjustments in their lives in order to get and keep a job. It teaches the basics of reliability, punctuality, positive mindedness, and eagerness to work hard.

—∞—

Grassroot Soccer
Thomas S. Clark, MD, Cofounder and Chief Executive Officer
www.grassrootsoccer.org/

Grassroot Soccer uses the power and appeal of soccer to educate, inspire, and mobilize communities to stop the spread of HIV. It sends out soccer heroes to deliver the essential message about HIV prevention to at-risk youth around the world.

———

City Academy High School
Milo Cutter, Founder
www.cityacademy.org/

The first charter school in the nation, City Academy was established in St. Paul, Minnesota, in 1992 to provide a small school with small classes to students who were failing to learn in larger high schools. Founded by teachers and designed in close cooperation with the students, City Academy strives to create an academic environment that best enables students to learn and grow. All program offerings and learning material are tailored to individual student needs, based on academic assessment and performance. City Academy believes that the curriculum should fit the child, not the child the curriculum.

———

Gift of Life Bone Marrow Foundation
Jay Feinberg, Founder and Executive Director
www.giftoflife.org

Gift of Life is a donor organization, facilitating bone marrow, blood stem cell, and cord blood transplants for children and adults suffering from life-threatening illnesses. Recognizing that a patient's best chance of finding a genetic match depends on locating donors of similar ethnicity, Gift of Life has made a special effort to increase the representation of Jewish donors—long undercounted—in the national bone marrow registry.

_᠆ᢙ_

Shape Up Vicksburg
Linda Fondren, Founder
www.shapeupvicksburg.com

A grassroots movement, Shape Up Vicksburg has strived to make Vicksburg, Mississippi, the fittest city in the nation. When the organization was founded in 1996 (originally as Shape Up Sisters, an all-women's gym), two-thirds of its residents were obese or overweight. Shape Up's goal is to end this epidemic and help citizens become and stay healthy through free fitness and nutrition programs.

_᠆ᢙ_

Art for Refugees in Transition
Sara M. Green, Founder and Executive Director
www.artforrefugees.org

A.R.T. offers curriculum and training programs to engage both children and adults in refugee communities in visual, performing, and creative arts drawn from their own cultures. These activities provide local and international relief institutions with the means of helping refugee communities recover from the traumas of war and natural disaster.

_᠆ᢙ_

KaBOOM!
Darell Hammond, Founder and Chief Executive Officer
http://kaboom.org/
KaBOOM! is a national nonprofit dedicated to saving play for America's children. It does so by organizing communities to build playgrounds in underserved areas. The goal: providing a place to play within walking distance of every child in America.

—☙

Genocide Intervention Network
(Now merged with Save Darfur Coalition to form United to End Genocide)
Mark Hanis, Cofounder
www.genocideintervention.net
www.endgenocide.org
Genocide Intervention Network started the world's first movement to end genocide and mass atrocities. It does this through political advocacy, providing protection for endangered groups in ongoing conflicts, and by pushing for prosecution of genocidal criminals.

—☙

Agahozo-Shalom Youth Village
Anne Heyman, Founder
www.agahozo-shalom.org/home.html
The Agahozo-Shalom Youth Village (ASYV) is a residential community in rural Rwanda that provides a home, a school, and a place of refuge for youth who were orphaned during and after the

genocide in 1994. Its 144 acres offer a place of hope, where "tears are dried" (signified by the Kinyarwanda word *agahozo*) and where the aim is to live in peace (*shalom* in Hebrew).

───

VisionSpring
Jordan Kassalow, Founder and Chief Executive Officer
www.visionspring.org/home/home.php

VisionSpring has created an entrepreneurial sales network that delivers highly durable, low-cost glasses to millions of sight-impaired people in the developing world. And with clear sight comes fresh hope to escape poverty and make a better life.

───

Harlem Village Academies
Dr. Deborah Kenny, Founder and Chief Executive Officer
www.harlemvillageacademies.org/

Harlem Village Academies (HVA) is a group of charter schools with an ambitious vision for its students: "to become intellectually sophisticated, wholesome in character, avid readers, independent thinkers, and compassionate individuals who lead reflective and meaningful lives." Rooted in the belief that teachers, not programs, largely determine student achievement, HVA set out to design a school where teachers are central to the enterprise. They are trusted as professionals, empowered to make important pedagogical decisions, and held accountable for the results.

───

The Messages Project
Carolyn LeCroy, Founder
http://themessagesproject.org/
What happens to the children left behind when a parent is incarcerated? The goal of the Messages Project is to maintain, or rebuild, the connection between imprisoned parents and their children through recorded video messages.

—◌

Health Leads (formerly Project HEALTH)
Rebecca Onie, Cofounder and Chief Executive Officer
www.healthleadsusa.org/
Health Leads connects energetic undergraduate volunteers with providers in urban clinics, to provide low-income patients with the basic resources, such as food, housing, and heating assistance, they need to be healthy.

—◌

Second Chance
Scott H. Silverman, Founder and former President
www.secondchanceprogram.org/
Second Chance gives the down-and-out a chance at self-sufficiency by providing job readiness training, employment placement, affordable housing, and life skills.

—◌

David Suzuki Foundation
Dr. David Suzuki, Cofounder
www.davidsuzuki.org/

The Foundation brings together government, business, and individuals to help protect the environment through science education, advocacy, policy work, and efforts to promote environmental awareness and action. The Foundation believes that the diversity of nature is the key to our quality of life.

—☙—

Many of the nonprofits you'll read about have had stunning impact: for example, Michael Brown has drawn over fifteen thousand students to take a break from their studies and give of themselves to be mentors and teachers with City Year. With KaBOOM!, Darell Hammond started what is now a widespread movement to bring together communities around the building of playgrounds. Mark Hanis was the first to mobilize a political force to combat genocide with his Genocide Intervention Network. Now internationally famous, Geoffrey Canada built a community-wide superstructure to support the underserved students of his Harlem Children's Zone. All of these accomplishments are astonishing, and just about all of them have been made with little to no money by ordinary people without any resources beyond their ingenuity. A student, a housewife, a high school graduate, an ex-con, a recovering addict—these are the sorts of individuals who started the nonprofits in this book, using only their ideas and their energy. But this combination has proven potent enough for these people to draw to them everything they've needed to see their ideas through: capital, staffing, technology, and connections. It is not magic, but it sometimes feels like it. Many of these entrepreneurs sensed their ideas pulling *them* along, not the other way around. These were ideas that were determined to be.

Who We Are

We, the authors of this book, are social entrepreneurs in spirit. Before coming to the Andrea and Charles Bronfman Philanthropies, Jeff Solomon created a number of innovative programs under the umbrella of the two large human service networks he headed. Charles Bronfman's foundation, the Andrea and Charles Bronfman Philanthropies, of which Jeff is the president, has guided the creation of a dozen start-ups in three countries, most famously Birthright Israel, a program that has already exposed more than three hundred thousand young Jewish adults to life in Israel for ten days, all expenses paid; 21/64, a program that fosters an intergenerational approach to strategic philanthropy; and the Historica-Dominion Institute, the leading NGO focused on Canadian history and heritage. One of the more interesting experiments of the Foundation was designed by Charles's late wife, Andrea, a few days after the tragedy of 9/11, and then enacted by Jeff. Rather than simply provide charitable monetary contributions to the families who lost loved ones, Andy and Jeff sought to find a way to help them to heal. They arranged for every one of the arts, cultural, entertainment, and sports venues in the tri-state area to provide free tickets to those in grief. The hope was that a museum, a baseball game, or a circus would help a grieving child find a reason to smile. Andy and Jeff built the Gift of New York to execute this idea and opened it by Christmas 2001—and they closed it, as planned, on Easter Sunday 2003. Ten thousand people took advantage of the program.

Because of our backgrounds, both of us, Jeff and Charles, have found that social entrepreneurs have increasingly sought us out for guidance and support as they embark on this most difficult quest, to create their own nonprofit. This book is drawn largely from what we have learned from and told these founders. It is the advice

12

we would give you, as a would-be founder, if we had a chance to sit down with you. We would relish a frank talk about what you need—both in yourself and from others—as you embark on this quest. And we are imagining that you would relish it, too. There are few more challenging or more fascinating endeavors than the one you are undertaking, and fewer still offer greater exhilaration when you reach your goal.

We come to this task from different backgrounds, but to both of us, nonprofits are, along with the government, the economy, and the press, the fourth leg of the stool that supports a decent life for our citizens and others around the world.

A Quick Tour

We think of this book as a do-gooder's handbook, if you use the definition of do-gooder from the Preface. It provides essential instruction to people like you—would-be social entrepreneurs who are thinking of starting a nonprofit or who have already begun one and are starting to wonder what they have gotten themselves into. It is not a textbook, nor is it some windy essay or a thorny legal treatise. Enlivened by the stories of the eighteen founders that form its core, it is meant to be a commonsense guide to this critical, often underappreciated, realm of human endeavor.

For much of this book, we will follow the life cycle of the nonprofit, starting with that first explosive Aha! moment of inspiration, and continuing with the intense process of self-examination in which you, as a potential founder, decide if you have the right stuff for this. Can you put your hands on the resources you'll need? Recruit and manage staff on a tight budget? Determine the plan and develop measures and systems? After your nonprofit has taken off, as the founder you'll need to change hats. Once the organization is sufficiently established and doesn't need to be grown much more, you'll need to become more a manager than an entrepreneur. In Part Three, we'll lay out the issues that the prudent manager needs to keep in mind, such as resource development, board governance issues, personnel matters, and, trickiest of all, Founder's Syndrome. Then we'll try to help with the largest question of all: when, and whether, to step aside and leave the work to others to carry on.

PART ONE

Sources of Inspiration

CHAPTER 1

That Aha! Moment

When Inspiration Strikes

THE INSPIRATION FOR A WONDERFUL NONPROFIT can come to you at any time. Indeed, it can be so capricious that social entrepreneurs sometimes joke that it was rather inconvenient, interrupting their plans not just for the day but for the decade or more. And it is true: a great nonprofit idea takes over. It keeps its own schedule. For you as the seeker of these novel, earth-shaking ideas, it is a matter of opening yourself to the unexpected, of letting go of your analytical capacity—that fabled, overworked left brain—and putting your faith in your underutilized creative side.

The best nonprofit ideas are off the beaten path, and they can shake you up a little. At forty-three, Anne Heyman was the mother of three young boys and thought of herself as an Upper West Side housewife when she decided to start a youth village for orphans in Rwanda, a place she had never been. Darell Hammond was twenty-two and just a high school graduate when he was struck by the idea that all children should have a playground close to home, and has dedicated his life to organizing local communities to build those playgrounds, thereby strengthening the communities themselves. Whether to Rwanda or the world of play, both of them found that their work took over their lives. With Heyman, she came to feel that she was always focused on Rwanda, regardless of whether she was there physically. And Hammond became a kind of play-master,

17

developing expertise in the psychology of playgrounds even as he struggled to find the funds for new playground construction. Regardless of whether they have been at their nonprofits for one year or twenty, few of the eighteen social entrepreneurs we profile in this book have any plans to change. They're lifers. A single burst of inspiration can change your life. It will create your life's work, almost whether you want it to or not.

Creativity in the nonprofit arena is often said to come "out of the blue," or to be, as someone might say with a puzzled shrug, "a total fluke." But on closer examination, there is usually a certain deep logic to it. Indeed, it often seems as though those struck by this kind of creativity were primed for that moment of brilliant insight by various events and relationships or ideas they've been exposed to throughout their lives, only they didn't know it. They have the idea because it fits them. And that will likely be true for you, too. The idea grows out of your experience, outlook, and personality. It is rooted in your life story, your philosophy, your aspirations. It is a seed within you that has come to flower as an expression of yourself, possibly the truest expression of yourself. For virtually all of these eighteen social entrepreneurs, building a nonprofit is, outside of their family lives, the most intensely personal thing they have ever done. It will probably be no less for you.

Truth to tell, in philanthropy as elsewhere, the truly transformative ideas are rare. Pedestrian ones, alas, are all too common. (If it were otherwise, the world would be a far finer place than it is.) The best ideas, however, are somehow organic, and they grow bigger the more you think about them. It can take a little while to see their full dimensions. That can be a way to tell just how good the idea is. The best ones expand like a gas, and they have a lift to them. And that lift creates a chain reaction, inspiring other ideas to make the big one happen. To the most astute, the inspiration doesn't come as an intellectual concept, one that is easily expressed in words, but as a full blasting vision, showing with startling clarity how the world is about to be.

Jordan Kassalow: Finding Vision

It can be staggering, that first moment of inspiration. Jordan Kassalow was training to be an optometrist when he had the experience that changed his life. Or two experiences, really, for the first made the second all the more meaningful. When he was young, Kassalow did a lot of mountain climbing, and one summer he joined a couple of friends in climbing in the Brooks Range of mountains in Alaska. It rained heavily as the three of them ascended to the peak, but they reached the summit safely. The rain was slashing sideways, driven by gale-force winds, and the two others retreated to the tent, but Jordan took a seat on a rock "in a very meditative state," he said, "just becoming one with the universe, if you will." But sitting there in the fierce rainstorm, he was also disturbed to sense that, as he says, "the universe was conspiring against me, and it was telling me I was just dust in the wind, and that I didn't really matter in the grand scheme of things." Affronted, Kassalow stood up and, for reasons he can't now recall, he started yelling back at the wind, "I do matter! I do!"

That Lear-like moment was a prelude to the second event six months later that proved to be even more pivotal. Along with some other students and professors of optometry, Kassalow was providing eye care to poor people in the Mexican outback. His very first patient was a seven-year-old boy whose vision was so blurred and indistinct that he was placed in a school for the blind. In that part of Mexico, the families of the blind suffer a double burden. Besides the distress of raising a blind child, they are likely to be ostracized in their community for bringing bad luck to the village.

Unsure what to make of this particular child's affliction, Kassalow brought him over to his professor, who examined the boy's eyes for a few minutes and then returned him to her student. "Jordan," she told him impatiently, "this boy isn't blind. This boy is just profoundly nearsighted." He had a prescription of over a minus 20, which is myopic to the absolute extreme. Kassalow recalls,

> We had brought down five thousand pairs of glasses, categorized by strength. And she said, "Go to the strongest box and see if there's anything that's remotely close to what this guy needs." And I did, and sure enough, there was a pair of glasses that was very close to his prescription. And so I was the one who put these glasses on this boy's face. And as the lenses aligned with his eyes, his whole face changed from the blank countenance of a blind person to this beautiful, animated smile of joy of a seven-year-old boy. I was the first person he ever saw in his life. And I remember at that moment looking up and saying to the heavens, "See? I do matter."

And that is the moment it came to him. He would do for thousands, tens of thousands, maybe hundreds of thousands of poor people around the world what he had just done for this one boy. He would bring glasses to the masses. He would let the world see.

Rachel Andres: Making Connections That Save Lives

Call them sparks, or lightning bolts—the best of these ideas all have a crackling, high-voltage quality, and, like electricity, they are burning for something to do. When the bold, transformative idea came to her, Rachel Andres was a forty-four-year-old Los Angeles–based

project consultant for Jewish World Watch (JWW), an organization dedicated to preventing another holocaust, and she did not
think of herself as a particularly creative person. Her job was to
raise awareness of the plight of the women survivors of the Darfur
genocide. This was 2006, and the world was just beginning to
focus on the genocide in Darfur. JWW took the lead in focusing
public attention on the thousands of people fleeing their homes in
Sudan for the relative security of vast makeshift camps across the
border in Chad.

Janice Kamenir-Reznik, the JWW's cofounder and president,
delivered a moving speech that year at Andres's synagogue in Los
Angeles about the plight of Darfuri refugees. Horrified by the
devastation and suffering, Andres was eager to help. Kamenir-
Reznik hired her to organize an event highlighting the horrendous
situation the surviving women and girls had endured—and maybe
to find a project JWW could support, too.

One idea was to raise funds to build a rape counseling center
in one of the camps, but that didn't feel right to Andres. Although
counseling was necessary for the recovery of the women, the whole
notion of a counseling center seemed too "Western" if the women
and girls still needed basic food, water, and safety for survival. Plus,
Andres wanted to concentrate on prevention, not treatment. She
realized that the camps weren't entirely safe for these refugees, and
in some ways they posed their own hazards. The cooking situation,
for instance. Virtually all the food supplied by the UN—beans,
macaroni, rice—needed to be cooked in the traditional manner on
a three-stone wood fire, as there was no gas or electricity. But that
required firewood, and, for each family, the monthly allotment
from the UN lasted only a week. When it was gone, the mother or
daughter often had to venture outside the camp to search for more.
Outside the confines of the camp, however, lurked vicious Sudanese
militia who preyed on any number of the women, raping them.

To Andres, the prospect of these refugees' being attacked again as they scavenged for firewood was unbearable. It had to be stopped—but how? By a complete coincidence, a JWW volunteer had been researching solar cooking for a book, and he thought it might work in the camps at Darfur. Andres hardly knew what a solar cooker was, but it seemed somehow right, and she could not get it out of her mind. Instead of cooking with firewood, the women would cook their food with sunshine. There was certainly no shortage of that in Africa! Instead of venturing out into the hazardous bush, the women could remain safely in camp to do their cooking. It was so simple, it was ingenious.

Andres Googled "Darfur solar cooker" and discovered a small pilot project in Chad using five hundred solar cookers for the eighteen thousand Darfuri refugees there. But who provided them? The first Web sites she found gave no clue. Instead they drew Andres into what she called a "little maze," with many wrong turns and backtracks, until she turned up an eccentric Dutchman named Dr. Derk Rijks. He had created a program for the refugees through an American organization called Solar Cookers International. After many emails, Andres was finally able to reach Rijks by phone. He described the "CooKit" solar cooker model he was using. It could hardly have been more basic: two flaps of cardboard, both of them covered with reflective tinfoil to focus the sun's rays, and a black pot underneath for the cooking.

Rijks welcomed Andres's assistance. He did not have the capability at that time to expand the program, but Andres hoped JWW could help him drastically increase his output to provide all the families in the camp with solar cookers. Maybe they could even outfit all of the dozen refugee camps in Chad.

Andres was a project consultant, with an emphasis on community relations and conference organizing. It was not in her job description to start a massive project to bring solar cooking to

Darfuri refugees. But if JWW was trying to build support for the refugees, she reasoned, this was a more enticing approach than just organizing another conference. It was clear to her that this was a project that might well attract donors, especially female donors. She figured they would be saving lives, one by one. So she set her goal at providing two solar cookers for every family in the camps—enough to cook a full meal.

The key to the success of the program was the price, and this was Andres's other insight. The elements of a cooker (and its delivery) were all simple enough—the cardboard, the tinfoil, the shipping, the ground transportation, the supervision. But they added up. To how much? It took much discussion through calls and emails to Rijks and his various suppliers to find out. Rijks himself did not know how much the cookers cost, but by pricing out the various elements and adding them up, Andres came up with a serviceable number: $30 per cooker. Andres could imagine the pitch: for $30 you can keep a Darfuri woman in the refugee camps and reduce her chances of rape and attack. (Or you could turn the page, in the words of a similar magazine pitch from years ago.) To donors, the pitch was irresistible—and it redounded to the credit of JWW, too.

Over five years later, in 2012, more than eleven thousand people have contributed financially—at synagogues and churches, in schools and offices—many of them giving $30, $60, $90, and other multiples of $30 from there. And although the price has now risen to $40 per cooker due to inflation, the progress continues. Four camps holding over ninety thousand people have been served with enough cookers to provide one to each family, and another three camps are about to be added, with seventy thousand people more.

And the results for the Darfuri women? According to a study by the JWW, before the cookers arrived, virtually every woman in the camp had to leave to hunt for firewood at least once a week, and often far more frequently than that. Since the arrival of the cookers, half of them never leave the camp at all. And those who do, leave far less often. Altogether, trips outside the confines of the camp had been reduced by 86 percent.[1] The JWW was not able to determine the resulting decrease in rape and attack, but it is fair to assume that it was roughly commensurate.

It is quite a story, this tale of a woman in Los Angeles who, on the strength of a single idea, saved countless women and girls of the refugee camps in Chad from rape and violence.

But, of course, these bursts of insight, these Aha! moments, are just the beginning, never the end. For the real power of such inspiration is never felt just by the individual who experienced it. It is passed like a pulse of electricity along filaments that proceed in every direction, lighting up the public, potential donors, staffers, board members, and countless others as it goes charging forth through the universe.

Carolyn LeCroy: Making Good of a Bad Situation

Not all moments of inspiration are so uplifting. Sometimes they come out of a period of disquiet, a bad time that allows in a certain soulfulness that is otherwise kept at bay. In these cases, the charitable effort isn't so much inspired as it is empathic, allowing the creator to see life from the point of view of someone with whom she would otherwise have no connection. It can take darkness to see the light.

That was true for Carolyn LeCroy. She was a freelance television producer in Norfolk, Virginia, when she made the mistake of a lifetime and got nailed for it. She let her ex-boyfriend stash what he called "some stuff" in her storage unit. She had a vague idea what the stuff might be, but figured it would be gone in a couple of days, so it wasn't worth worrying about. Unfortunately, the police came through the area with drug-sniffing dogs on another matter, and they went wild over the "stuff" of LeCroy's ex. It proved to be a good-sized bale of marijuana, well over the five pounds that constitutes a felony under Virginia law. Facing charges of possession with intent to distribute, plus conspiracy, she was found guilty and sentenced to fifty-five years. "When I heard that, my knees buckled," she remembers. "My attorney reached for me, because he thought I was going under, and two sheriffs came up to grab my arms. I went into complete shock. I'd never had as much as a parking ticket, and now this?"

Happily, all but six years of her sentence were almost immediately suspended, and, with parole and time off for good behavior, she ended up serving just fourteen months in the Virginia Correction Center for Women. "When you say 'just,'" she protests, "as in 'just fourteen months,' that may make sense compared to someone serving twenty-five years, but *you* try serving one day in prison, just one."

It was a long hitch, but one thing made it seem shorter: regular visits from her two sons, David and Mike, then nineteen and twenty-four. They came to visit her a couple of weekends a month, and Carolyn wasn't sure she could have gotten through her time without them. She noticed that a large number of the other women never had any visitors at all, and it was awful. "I saw depression," she recalls. "I saw hurt. I saw anger. And then they get pissed off at you because you got company, and you were in a good mood."

"And I thought about that and I thought about that," but it wasn't until she was finally freed from prison and was speaking to her younger son, David, that the penny dropped. She asked him, "If I could have given you anything from prison, what would it be?" And he looked at her dead-on and said, "You."

25

"And that," she says, "is when it hit me." The idea came not as a concept, but as an image. Two images, actually: "Of a woman in front of a camera in prison, and of her children watching her at home." Thus began the Messages Project.

Some of the time, the children didn't want to come to the prison, but more often they simply couldn't, because the distance was too great and they had other obligations. But the video of Mom or Dad would come to them from prison, as if delivered by Netflix. "If the kids can't get to the moms, what about the moms getting to kids?" LeCroy asked herself. She would use her skill as a film producer to create videos of these women talking to their children, and then send the videos to them. At the very least, the children could see that their mother was fine. Beyond that, they might be able to still feel the love.

"It was very simple," LeCroy says. A video camera, a videotape, a tripod, a camera operator, an interviewer, and that would be it. Out of prison, she wrote to the Virginia Department of Corrections asking for permission to put her idea into effect. She got major support from one of the principals in the prison schools, and, at his recommendation, she had included some statistics on the connection between the maintenance of the parent–child bond and a decrease in the likelihood that the child would become an inmate. As it was, the child of a convicted felon is six to ten times more likely to end up in prison than other children, which was a key part of her argument. And LeCroy can understand some of the reasons why: children of prisoners are traumatized by the separation; they feel abandoned, unloved, and guilty, as if they themselves were responsible for their parent's incarceration. "But if you can reestablish the bond, you see a huge difference in the behavior. Once they actually hear Mom say, 'I didn't abandon you. This was not your fault. I love you. Don't go down this road. Let me tell you where it leads.' It's one thing to write this down in a letter, but it's another if the child can actually see his mom saying these things. It's a huge difference. Because you cannot hide from the camera's eye. You can't fake the body language or conceal the facial expressions."

LeCroy received permission from the warden, and it looked like she was in: she would go into Fluvanna Correctional Center for Women, a maximum-security facility for violent offenders—women convicted of murder, attempted murder, vicious assaults, and the like. Despite the ferocity of these crimes, the warden was unusually progressive; she could see the benefits of the program and wasn't put off by the security issues posed by a video camera. LeCroy would produce her first set of videos in time for Christmas. She had twenty-seven inmates lined up to send messages to their loved ones. But just five days before the shoot, a top administrator said no. Permission revoked. No explanation given.

"Now, anyone who knows me knows I have the tenacity of a pit bull," says LeCroy. It is a characteristic that is widely shared among social entrepreneurs, who become immune to the word no. An important first lesson: if you are not assertive and accept rejection easily, do not pursue social entrepreneurship! "With me, until the very last door is closed and locked and nailed shut, I'm going to keep trying to get in." So she kept at it. She shifted her sights to Mother's Day, which was the birthday of her older son, Michael, so it seemed propitious. And this time, permission was granted and stayed granted.

For this one, seventy-five women signed up, and, one by one, they filed into the makeshift studio for their cameos. LeCroy had a cameraman and an assistant, but she was the director, the reassurer-in-chief, and the one ready with the Kleenex when things got emotional. To preserve the women's privacy, she refused to have any guards standing by; she would take her chances with her own safety. (She never once felt endangered.) A group of students from the prison's school of cosmetology helped do the women's hair and makeup. Each video ran fifteen minutes. Some of the prisoners spoke directly from their heart and into the camera. Others relied on notes to remember everything they wanted to be sure to say. Others read from the "gently loved" children's books that LeCroy provided and could send home with the video. Many of them tearfully showed off the pictures they had of their children, to show that they still had them in their lives, every day. The male prisoners generally avoided openly showing feelings, until they got in front of the camera and the hard shell came off. One brought a basketball to demonstrate his jump shot; another taught his son how to tie his shoes. All of them, it was clear, had been desperate to connect with their children.

When the videos arrived in the mail, there were many reports of enthralled kids cuing them up to watch the videos again and again: the flickering image on the TV screen the closest they would get to Mom or Dad. The books their moms or dads read on video were treasured by the children, often ending up under their pillows at night.

The media attention was overwhelming. Newspapers and local TV shows covered it, and NPR did a story on *All Things Considered*. "It was incredible the amount of press coverage we got," says LeCroy. One of the particular delights was seeing some of the bureaucrats who had turned her down so harshly do an about-face once they saw how much publicity they could gain for their institutions, and for themselves, by getting involved. LeCroy expanded her efforts from one prison to three, but it became exhausting. LeCroy and her cameraman contributed their time, including the considerable travel time, but each video cost $10, making it $750 for that first crop of messages. Not knowing where else to turn for the money, LeCroy paid for that first set herself. The next set would pose a problem.

For LeCroy, as for the others, the beginning is just the beginning. Much more lay ahead, and each step of the process involves a winnowing to create laserlike focus. Just to get a nonprofit launched is an accomplishment, and compelling testimony to the power of the idea and to the talents and inspiration of the founder. Still, as LeCroy was discovering as she maxed out her credit card, it is one thing to get a nonprofit up, and it is quite another to keep it running.

The Best Ideas Combine the Familiar with the Unexpected

The strength of a truly winning idea comes from the combination of its novelty and familiarity, which often involves taking a familiar concept and using it in an unexpected context or setting. In psychology, this is called lateral thinking. You take an idea from column A and join it to one from column B. If the new pairing is truly fresh, it can unleash startling energy—if, that is, it is novel enough to be arresting, practical enough to be effective, yet simple enough to be almost immediately graspable. It has to be clear what the idea is. Everybody knows glasses—Kassalow's inspiration was in placing the emphasis on the sight-deprived in developing countries. And videos are familiar enough—they were new only as a medium for the messages from prisoners to their children. A solar cooker was more inventive, but it was easily understood. Andres's brilliance was in bringing them to the camps at Darfur. The ease of explanation is always key to any marketing effort. The best pitches are the ones that the customer makes herself.

It all starts with one person and grows from there. For all three of these social enterprises, it was no easy matter to scale up, to move from one cooker to many, from one pair of glasses to hundreds of thousands, from one prison in Virginia to several throughout the country. In the case of Kassalow, it took fifteen years. Much of the energy for that effort comes from the idea itself, if the idea is powerful enough, but the rest has to come from the person. These brilliant innovations, after all, are just ideas or visions. If the founder has a personal connection to the work, as LeCroy, Andres, and Kassalow all did and most founders do, he or she will bring yet another pocket of energy to the endeavor. In the end, it's caring and passion that make the effort so explosive.

But passion alone will not make for a brilliant nonprofit. Any enthusiasm has to be checked by a skepticism that proceeds from the inside out. It is not enough to go wild over an idea; you'll need to let it rattle around in your head as you ask yourself, *Will this really work? Does anybody need this? Can I possibly find the resources to accomplish this? Am I up to it? Is it worth it?* And even—*Is it safe? Will it, as the physicians say, do no harm?* Next, check with friends and family members to see if they share your enthusiasm. And then go outward from there to nonprofit professionals and specialists in the field. Excitement is one thing, but realism is another. If you are the only one who believes in your idea, you should probably shelve it and wait for another one to come along that grabs others, too.

CHAPTER 2

The Prequel

The Backstory:
The History Behind the Idea

IN HOLLYWOOD, EVERY STORY HAS A BACKSTORY—the story behind the story that adds not just a historical dimension but often a complex psychological one as well, as it explains how that main story came to be. The backstory gives the front story the depth and resonance that ultimately provides its true meaning.

As in Hollywood, so in nonprofits. The story behind the story can give its host institution, an otherwise soulless entity, its emotional power. The backstory goes behind the stated mission to explain how that mission came to be, and that can explain everything. For the concepts behind the best of the nation's nonprofits are never generic, the product of some market survey. They're intensely personal, generally arising in a moment of nearly religious intensity. However they might be experienced, they aren't truly bolts from the blue, coming out of nowhere, but rather upsurges of deep feeling that arise from what might be thought of as the founder's innermost self. Yet for all their individuality, they depend for their impact on a rare kind of sympathy that forges a link between the founder's own struggles and those of others. Like all the best philanthropy, these acts connect soul to soul.

Scott H. Silverman: Using the Past to Help Others Find a Future

Take Scott H. Silverman, the tough-minded founder of a remarkably successful rehabilitation program called Second Chance. Based in downtown San Diego, it has taken hundreds of convicts, drug addicts, alcoholics, and the homeless and sought to turn their lives around, overcoming the addictions, ending the self-defeating behaviors, finding jobs for those willing and able to work, and providing shelter for the homeless. City programs have mostly given up on these lost souls; Second Chance is about the only agency willing to give them a shot. It's a thriving organization with several dozen employees now, but in the early days, Second Chance was basically just Scott. Imposing, hilarious, relentlessly positive minded, he devoted himself to his wayward charges seven days a week. "I was the point person, the hand holder, the mentor, the career coach, the life coach, the disciplinarian," he says. "The parent, really."

Why? The backstory explains everything, because he was himself one of those lost souls. Silverman in his thirties was himself secretly "poly-addicted" to just about every kind of drug, but chiefly alcohol. Still, he was somehow able to hold a job in the family clothing firm, own a home, get married, travel for business, and carry on—until November of 1984, when it all came crashing down. One evening, when he was in New York on business, he started in on a bender and didn't stop until he passed out dead drunk on a city sidewalk two days later. The police peeled him off the sidewalk and, finding a key in his pocket, returned him to his hotel. "The staff put me on a luggage rack and wheeled me up to my room and just kind of plopped me on the bed," he says. The next morning he woke up in his clothes. He had no memory of the night before.

He was supposed to have a breakfast meeting with a group of wholesalers downtown. He arrived far too late for the meeting, so he asked a showroom manager to point him to an empty office to make a call—but actually to stall for time. It had been over two days since anyone had heard from him. He was sweating, panicky, and hopeless, and he decided that the best thing for everyone would be for him to open the window, climb out onto the window ledge, and take things from there. "It was just to catch my breath," he says. "But that's when I realized there's an opportunity here. If I just leaned over and pushed myself out the window, I wouldn't have to explain anymore to anybody what had been going on with my behavior." It was the forty-fourth floor. The cars looked very small way down below, and he could barely hear the honking. He inched his body out, ever closer to tipping out into oblivion. "I was prepared to end my life," he says solemnly. "I was saying good-byes in my head."

But just then the executive who used that office came in and saw Silverman perched like a gargoyle on the window sill. "What the hell are you doing?" he shouted. "For Christ's sake, climb down from there." Too startled to do anything but comply, Silverman stepped down. Once he was safely inside, he broke down and called his wife.

A "divine intervention," Silverman calls that man who saved his life.

Since then, for countless other people, the divine intervention would be Silverman himself.

That morning might have been the end, but it proved to be the beginning, setting him on course to create Second Chance for down-and-outers like himself. It was a long road back, largely because he had gone a long way out. "That was a major life-changing event," he says. "I had gotten to a point where I could not live with the insanity that I had brought on myself and my family." He flew back to San Diego, and the next day he entered a treatment program for his addictions. "I realized I was drinking because I was depressed, and I was depressed because of my drinking," he says. He has not had a drink since that day, November 13, 1984.

He often tells the story of his near-suicide at workshops and to individuals in need. "I use whatever I can to hopefully inspire, motivate, open minds and hearts, and create some hope and passion and faith. Maybe it will capture someone so they won't get to the forty-fourth floor themselves," he says, then adds: "I don't think we honor life-changing events like that enough. When you look at most people who are so passionate about something"—people like himself, he means—"that they're devoting countless hours to it, it's usually about something that happened with them, for them, to them, or around them." They are ministering to themselves.

By tapping into that core identity, Silverman has touched the real. And there lies a lesson for all founders, for the best nonprofits are all rooted in such fundamental experiences. Without such a visceral connection, as a founder you will find that it is all too easy to lose sight of your convictions when the temptation comes to alter your mission to satisfy a donor or catch a trend.

The treatment program offered Silverman something else. Not just a new lease on life, but something important to do in it. He found an exuberance he'd never felt before except under the influence. When the staff saw how outgoing he was, they thought to make use of it by naming him a patient rep, the one who greets the new patients and welcomes them into the group. "Busy hands are happy hands, you know," Silverman says cheerfully. He was hooked. When he emerged from treatment, he returned as a volunteer—putting in four thousand hours over the next four years, an astounding figure. "I was very committed to helping others," he says, "If you help others, you help yourself."

Like Kassalow with his glasses, LeCroy with her prison messages, and countless other founders of change-making nonprofits, Silverman discovered his mission as a response to his own moment of revelation. The experience itself dictated the course of his life. He didn't choose it; it was simply inevitable. And that inevitability carried with it a rightness that he found not just inescapable but that he needed to pass on to others. It was like a conversion experience, and he became an evangelical. Silverman preached rehab.

He zeroed in on his work at Second Chance when he volunteered in a local program through his temple, called the Hunger Project. Eager to branch out from a narrow conception of treatment, Silverman wanted to get into a line of healing that captured more of his rebirth experience on that New York window ledge. The transformation, after all, wasn't just chemical; it was far more spiritual. Likewise, the Hunger Project did not address literal hunger, but the metaphorical variety. The project was popular, but most people left the volunteering to an occasional Sunday. After the first Sunday, Silverman went every single Sunday thereafter, without fail. He loved it, and his clients loved him. After three months, the head of volunteers came up to him and asked how he could explain the amazing rapport he seemed to have with so many people in the program.

"It's because I know them," he replied. "Just not personally." After all, he'd been on the receiving end of such care. He could talk to drug dealers for the same reason, persuading a gang of them to push on, and leave a certain neighborhood alone. Why? Same reason: he'd been a drug dealer himself, selling to get money to buy. "I knew the customer," he explains. He'd been one.

His background widened his rapport among the clients of the Hunger Project; he had a point of chemical connection with almost everyone. Pills, booze, weed—Silverman had been there. Many of the users kept coming back to this wise-cracking, middle-aged guy who seemed to really get them. So he started to press his advantage. "Why aren't you working?" he demanded. The excuses were varied, as were the barriers—one was on parole, another on probation, a third in recovery. To them all, Silverman said, "What if I helped you?" To his frustration, everyone just shrugged. No one would take him up on it.

Finally, he found a man who said he could use Silverman's help getting a job. Silverman did not go easy on him, pushing him harder than he had ever been pushed, for Silverman knew that any employer would go even harder. The man went away, discouraged, but reconsidered a couple of weeks later. Silverman did not ease off. "I'll help," Silverman told him. "But you have to be willing. Are you?"

The man nodded, "Yes, I am."

"How willing?" Silverman demanded.

"Totally," the man answered. "Totally willing."

Silverman stared at him a moment and then, like a drill sergeant, demanded that he drop down on the ground right there at his feet and give him ten, right now. The man was incredulous. "Ten push-ups?"

"Yes. Ten push-ups. Now." He pointed at the ground.

The man just stood there. "I'm not doing that."

"Then you're not willing."

"I'm not willing to do *that*." He stared at Silverman. "Why should I?"

"Because I asked. A job interviewer is going to ask you to do a helluva lot more than that, and if you give him the lip you just gave me, you'll be right out the door. Good-bye. You're not going to get that job. You're not going to get *any* job. So don't waste my time."

The man looked at Silverman in a new way. "Okay. Fine. I'll give you ten push-ups—but then you'll help me, right?"

"Absolutely."

The man bent down, reached toward the ground, and started to stretch himself out. Silverman told him to stop right there. "Stand up."

"But I haven't started yet."

"That's okay. You showed me you were willing. That's all you needed to do. Now I know I can help you, because you're willing to help yourself."

And Silverman did help him, and once word got out, people started gathering on Sundays for help from him. After about six months, he would routinely have thirty or forty people waiting for him when he arrived on Sunday. He worked a paying job the other six days, and, between this new career coaching and his original volunteering, he soon found himself working twelve hours on Sunday, too. Something had to give, and it was the paying job. He wanted to make his life, in effect, a week full of Sundays.

Like all the genesis myths of these founders, there is always a beginning before the beginning. As it does in Silverman's case, the prequel usually offers the fullest explanation for how the nonprofit came to be, and why, and for whom. And, again as is true for Silverman, those answers are often to be found in the founder's own quest for healing or meaning or connection. If that quest leads to a satisfying discovery, then the founder is likely to want to share the good news with others, with all the urgency, excitement, and authenticity that come from lived experience. And these are the best emotions on which to base a nonprofit.

Deborah Kenny: A Better Way to Mourn

Personal tragedy is often the stimulant for seeking an outlet through doing good. For Deborah Kenny, the founder of what has become the Harlem Village Academies, her work has been an act of personal transformation that has turned into the transformation of the educational structure of Harlem. It was born in sadness in the aftermath of her husband's untimely death from leukemia. Unable to sleep in those early months of her grief, she would stay up reading books about the struggles of other suddenly single mothers, and that brought her to the works of the author Jonathan Kozol describing inner-city schools where so many single mothers congregated. Kenny realized that she herself had been blessed by an extended network of friends and family, whereas these other mothers had fewer resources. Kenny had been working at the publishing division of Sesame Workshop when her husband died, and she had a degree in comparative education from Columbia, but she did not know exactly where to turn when she developed this vague sense that she needed to do something for single women like her. But what, exactly?

She searched everywhere for the answer—battered women's shelters, abused children's organizations, parent training organizations, political advocacy groups. She concluded that underlying all of these social issues was one: education. An educated person is less likely to turn to crime or take drugs, and he or she is more likely to contribute to society than to be a drain on it. Access to quality education would address the needs and desires of single mothers at the most fundamental level. So she decided she would build a school in Harlem, a part of New York where she had never been.

It never occurred to her that it might be too difficult. "I think I've been blessed with confidence that was instilled in me by my parents," she says. Confidence was required, for every aspect of her new undertaking was daunting. "It was like everything you can imagine for starting a new business—then triple it." She had a school in mind, except that there were no charter schools back then, nor any charter center, nor any of the national models available today. Nor the conferences that are now rolled out seemingly every week to help neophytes get started. "Every single thing had to be figured out from scratch. How do you order supplies? How do you get insurance? How do you find a building? Technology? Legal advice?"

To get answers, she visited "dozens and dozens" of schools—private ones, primarily, as they tended to be better. One was Sidwell Friends in Washington DC, where the Obama daughters attend. She spent much of a year meeting people in the field. Although she was not anything close to a professional educator, she had been a teacher, a student before that, and a mother of three children who were then in middle school. So she had in mind what she calls a "very, very clear vision."

In all this effort, it was hard to prioritize the work. No single thing seemed vastly more important than anything else. One would think that getting the best teachers would be essential, and it was, but so was securing the right building, developing an appropriate curriculum, choosing an effective support staff, and everything else. Even so, Kenny didn't hire a single teacher without going to see him or her teach, even though that meant schlepping all over the city. Winning the good ones away was another problem. Given the tenure, pension, and job security issues, she could lure them only with her vision—a vision she hoped would be theirs—of more freedom to teach the way they wanted and believed was right, and less mindless bureaucracy to stand in their way. In many cases, although not all, that was enough.

For Kenny, the effort was stupendous, but when she is asked if she ever found it hard, putting together two schools from scratch, she professes not to understand the question. "Are you saying I was tired?" When the question is rephrased, listing the potential difficulties, she still doesn't get it. "What exactly are you asking?" she repeats. After a third attempt, she grants that the whole thing did take "a little bit of a toll" on her health. And, although it was exhausting, "I love it, and it's energizing, and it's sort of exhilarating and exhausting at the same time."

Darell Hammond: Your Past Is Never Behind You

Darell Hammond is the founder of KaBOOM!, which is not only the leading builder of playgrounds in the United States but has utterly transformed the way playgrounds get built in America. When KaBOOM! started in 1996, only 1 percent of all playgrounds were created by volunteers from the community, rather than by professional builders. Now 40 percent are. And this speaks to Hammond's success in accomplishing his goal of empowering communities to create change for themselves. "The idea was to use the playground as a Trojan horse to get the community to work together to complete a project on time," he explains. "We were less about the playground and more about the process." More about the community, in fact. Once energized, a community can go on from the playground to work together to improve local schools, health care, and other public services.

Hammond founded the company when he was twenty-three. Initially, when just a few playgrounds were being built at a time, he would move to the site of one of them and live there for a bit while the playground was being built. Almost like an anthropologist, he was curious to see the social consequences of the build. "I always thought we were creating social capital," he says. "The playground is a signal of and a metaphor for what can be accomplished when people come together."

In a way, the idea for the playgrounds came from Habitat for Humanity, the organization made famous by the involvement of President Jimmy Carter. "Habitat for Humanity wasn't really about housing," he points out. "It was about elevating the notion of substandard housing for all." Raising consciousness, one might say, along with roof beams. But KaBOOM! was born around the time of AmeriCorps and Walk for Hunger and a host of community service and corporate volunteer programs. So KaBOOM! was very much in tune with the zeitgeist.

Yet there was another element, one rather unexpected, that motivated him more profoundly than anything else. Along with his seven brothers and sisters, Hammond grew up in an orphanage, and he remained there for fourteen years. The experience left him eager for a community that was enriching rather than dispiriting. "I was fed, clothed, given an education," he says, "but I also had pretty low expectations for myself." It took some time for those expectations to rise. "I started KaBOOM! to create a place where people fight for something instead of against something." It was a way to counter the spirit of the orphanage. More, it was a matter of challenging both the community and the kids to bring out their best selves. Hammond thinks it is unfortunate that play is considered the opposite of work, because for kids, play is work. It is how they work out social relations, take risks, invent space, take on roles. He is especially intolerant of playgrounds that are "bubblewrapped to keep your kid from scraping a knee or skinning an ankle." Such risks, he says, are essential elements in play. "They bring out the toughness, resilience, and perseverance that come with life," he says. And this, too, might be traced back to his years in the orphanage, that academy of hard knocks.

Robert Carmona: Making the Most of Bitter Experiences

Robert Carmona, the cofounder of the outreach program now called STRIVE International, was a teenage drug addict in East Harlem, where the program is based, as well as a drug dealer, burglar, and, finally, in 1976, an armed robber. Sentenced to five years in prison, he was given the opportunity to opt out in favor of a therapeutic program called Daytop Village. He did it simply to avoid the lockup. "I didn't go there to change," he says. "I thought it would be easier." It made all the difference in his life. "It focused on an individual being able to own their disposition in life," he says, "and own the choices they made. It was a personal responsibility model." Rather than viewing themselves as victims of circumstance, they learned to see themselves as authors of their fate. For Carmona, that difference was everything.

After he completed his time in the program, three wealthy investors came to him with a stunning proposition. One of them was, says Carmona, "the quintessential WASP from Pittsburgh," a man named Sam Hartwell. He was married to a Vanderbilt, worked at Merrill Lynch, and volunteered at the Henry Street Settlement, a multiservice center on the Lower East Side of Manhattan. Another was Tom Rodman, another Henry Street volunteer, who worked for a financial firm. The third was the Henry Street executive director, Mike Fry. The settlement house had a workforce development component, and the three men had come to realize that it was set up all wrong. The training focused on job skills—typing, filing—that did indeed lead to employment. The problem was that the employment rarely lasted. Why? Because these employees lacked "soft skills"—all the character traits that can't easily be taught in a jobs program but are essential to success. Things like punctuality, cheerfulness, acceptance, and openness to criticism.

The three men came to Carmona because they figured that he was perfect to run the program they had in mind: Daytop Village had taught him these very values, he was from East Harlem, and he was an ex-con. He was an example of the transformation they sought to produce, and proof that it worked. So the deal was struck.

"When I started, I believed that if you see yourself as a victim, then you are a victim," he says. "You don't think you are empowered to control your life." That was his own life lesson, after all.

STRIVE started out in the basement of an East Harlem settlement house, staffed largely by ex-offenders, former substance abusers, or people who had had "skirmishes" with the law. "But all of us had pulled our lives together," he emphasizes. "So there was a built-in role-modeling function." And it clicked. There was a tightness with the clientele, a spreading belief in the program, and growing enthusiasm for the notion that, whatever the caricature of welfare slugs, men and women from East Harlem really wanted to work. Impressed with how things were going, Sam Hartwell brought Carmona to Pittsburgh to replicate the program there in the Three Rivers Employment Service. Then it was on to Chicago. The television program *60 Minutes* heard about STRIVE and gave it two of its three segments in a show in 1996, the year after Clinton signed welfare reform legislation. It was one of the highest-rated shows in the program's (then) twenty-eight-year history. The program has proliferated from there.

The motivation to do good comes from both the positive and the negative. Whether from uplifting experiences in their youth or from having to overcome personal challenges, the results were the impetus for these social entrepreneurs to want to help others.

Using Your Past to Create Change

There comes a time for all social entrepreneurs to decide which side of the great divide between for-profit and not-for-profit they are going to be on. If you're thinking about starting a nonprofit, it won't be an easy decision for you. It's a bit like deciding whether to go into the ministry—if not a monastery—for you'll be consigning yourself to a world that runs on principles entirely different from those of the so-called real world. No surprise here: there's no profit in nonprofits. Money is always in short supply, which means that everything is in short supply, as just about everything requires money—staff, equipment, office space, and, to some degree, you. Yet nonprofits have precious few ways of generating money. Banks are extremely reluctant to support an enterprise with no obvious source of revenue; your friends and family can't keep coughing it up; grantors and foundations aren't likely to support a fledgling project without a track record.

Starting a nonprofit is tough, which is another reason why you'll keep coming back to your personal story. It's like Genesis, the book that sets up everything in the Bible. Your story provides the core meaning, the source, the sense of purpose and much of the energy that will carry you through the many rough spots in the creation and running of a nonprofit. One of the biggest myths in the nonprofit world is that it is all about altruism, and populated only by saints. Hardly. A do-gooder is as selfish as the next guy. You do the work chiefly for yourself, for your highly personal definition of success and your own individual gratification, which just happen to come from service to others.

All the entrepreneurs discussed in this chapter and throughout the book come from different backgrounds, sometimes wildly different ones, just as for-profit entrepreneurs do. The difference between social entrepreneurs and their for-profit cousins is that the former rarely leave their pasts behind. Rather they mine them, if only subconsciously, for inspiration in their philanthropic endeavors. On some level, all recognize that by helping others, they help themselves, by making an unhappy experience into a lesson to others, or by simply making use of it. This is a theme we will return to time and again: the recognition that the founding entrepreneur and her life experiences are central to the enterprise in ways that go far beyond the role of her for-profit counterpart.

Obviously, for-profit entrepreneurs kill themselves for their start-up. But they don't draw on themselves emotionally nearly so much as the entrepreneurs you have met in this chapter, and many of the others to come. The for-profit entrepreneur stops at the border of her soul. Not so the social entrepreneur. She crashes on through.

PART TWO

Bringing Your Idea to Life

"Yes, but what are your goals?"

CHAPTER 3

What It Takes

Can You Really Do This?

So, WHAT DOES IT TAKE FOR YOU to bring a new nonprofit into the world, and do you have it? First it requires an arresting idea, one that combines novelty and familiarity in a way that creates excitement. But it also takes a profound emotional commitment from you, the founder. So, before you go much further with such an undertaking, you'll need to decide if you can stick with your day job, or jump. If the nonprofit takes off, you will have to take off with it. Do you really have time for this? Are you comfortable with the risk that it might not work out? Do you really want to give up so much of your life for this? Do you want to put your family through this? The short of it is that starting a nonprofit will dominate your life for at least the next three years, and if you really want to make a major impact, a full decade—and maybe even more.

You'll need to be honest with yourself in other ways, as you size yourself up as the prospective leader of a demanding, uncertain enterprise. Be honest: Do you have the skills you'll need to bring it off? Are you inventive—able to make more with less, to invoke a compelling future, to rally people to your cause? Are you disciplined—which is to say, can you say no, and mean it? Are you good with money—cost controls, revenue projections, interest rates? Are you good at asking for contributions? (You'll be doing a lot of that.) Asking your parents, other family members, friends?

Are you willing to put up your own money? Are you good with all sorts of people—from wealthy donors to high school interns, to say nothing of the recipients of your charity? Would you be just as comfortable sitting in the private dining room at the Gates Foundation as you are doing the Thursday night potluck at the Elks Club downtown? Not so easy, any of it, and it gets harder if your nonprofit fails to catch on.

Some other questions to seriously consider: Are you okay with doing everything pretty much all by yourself? Sometimes nonprofits are started by several partners, but not very often, and that may be just as well. Partners may not always agree, and it can be difficult to determine who should have final say. But if it is just you, you can find it a strain to decide everything by yourself, especially because you are likely to have only a few areas of deep expertise, at most, when dozens more are required to deal with everything from debt ratios to health benefits to accounting practices. You'll be like a baseball player who plays every position on the field and also manages the team.

To get right down to it, these are the hard questions you need to ask yourself:

1. Am I prepared to stay with this idea for ten years to make it happen? Do I have that attention span?
2. What role do I want for myself once the organization is up and running? Chief volunteer officer? Chief professional officer? If it's the first, my role is to set policy, but not enact it. If it's the second, I'll enact policy, but not set it. Which is more my style?
3. Are other organizations doing what I seek to do? Why am I not contributing to them?
4. What does my family think about this? Are they genuinely supportive? Do my friends think I'm crazy? To whom do I

turn for advice? Would they be part of my team of advisers? Am I ready to involve them in the decision about whether or not to go ahead? What if we disagree?

5. Do I know what I will do Day 1? Day 2? Week 2?

6. Am I disciplined? Will I give up a small victory now for a more major strategic gain later? Can I hold my tongue?

7. Am I mission driven or market driven? What sort of sacrifices am I prepared to make to see my idea through?

8. Can I work with others? Am I prepared to share credit? To take blame? Will I be generous with my assets, whether they are in the form of influence, money, or ideas?

9. Will I stick with it? Are setbacks likely to throw me off my game? Can I recover—and learn—from defeats? Am I an effective salesperson?

10. How am I as a team leader? Can I pick great team members, people who are passionate, talented, witty, vital, and smart? What are my priorities in personnel? Do I want yes-people? No-people?

11. How do I define success? Can I develop measures to determine if I have achieved it? Do I believe in "getting up to the balcony" to gain a broad view of everything going on? Or do I want to keep my feet on the ground? Can I handle financial reporting? Or know someone who does? Is all the hard work worth it to me? Will the satisfaction be worth the sacrifice?

12. How far will I go to pursue this idea? What risks am I prepared to take?

13. How do I feel about publicity? Would I be thrilled to be on *60 Minutes,* or terrified?

14. What is my exit strategy?

This is a very demanding job, and even the most altruistic and well-meaning person may not answer all these questions in the most positive way. But if you find yourself falling short on too many, you might ask yourself whether this nonprofit gambit really is for you.

But don't let us scare you off! Although creating a nonprofit may be hard, it can also be fantastically rewarding. Here, compensation is not measured in dollars. In performing a broad service to humanity, rather than merely generating revenue for a few, you create meaning, identity, and purpose for many. If you succeed, you'll make the world a better place, and how many people can say that?

Anne Heyman: Getting Things Up and Running

Like most founders, Anne Heyman embarked on her project of creating a Rwandan youth village pretty much without a clue. You'll see in her story just how sweeping your role as founder is likely to be, as every significant decision on just about every topic will probably fall to you, whether you are an expert in that area or not. An Upper West Side mother of three, Heyman was, at forty-two, a self-described "nothing" (despite a stint as assistant DA in Manhattan) when she happened to hear a lecture at Tufts University on the Rwandan genocide. "That's where I first learned about the orphan problem there," she says. Due to the Rwandan genocide and its aftermath, the country had over a million orphans. Heyman couldn't bear the thought of so many lost souls. "The moment I heard of it, literally, right then, it popped out of my mouth: 'They should build youth villages.'"

She thought so because, after the Holocaust, countless Jewish children had likewise been left without homes or families, and the new state of Israel had created youth villages for them. So why not do this in Rwanda for the Rwandan orphans? It would not only help the orphans but also, to the extent that it was perceived as a Jewish project, spread a positive image of Judaism throughout the world. As a South African native, Heyman certainly had a feeling for the special problems of Africa, but she had never been to Rwanda and had no expertise with orphaned children at all.

Nonetheless, she couldn't get the idea out of her head, so she started in, first by consulting all the experts she could find. "Everybody thought it was a brilliant idea," she says, but no one had much of a notion of how to bring it off, either. Here she demonstrated what separates nonprofit founders from normal people: this lack of a solution did not stop her. Nothing stopped her.

Heyman is not a moon shot sort of person. She is headstrong, no question, but also sensible, personable, and extremely focused. Although the prospect of starting a youth village in an inhospitable country that she had never visited was, shall we say, daunting, she worked to make it manageable. She proceeded, she says, "step-by-step," methodically developing her expertise in each new topic before proceeding. "It's not rocket science," she says. "You don't have to start from scratch." So it was by steady increments rather than in one bold swoop that she proceeded to recruit donors, develop a model of the village, work out the building plans, buy land, and assemble a small army of builders, village planners, psychologists, and educators. And now, just five years later, there stands in Rwanda a youth village for five hundred children, complete with a school, renewable energy, and marketable crops.

For her, it was all problem-solution, problem-solution, the work creating the method, rather than the other way around. "This was the way I learned to do things in law school," she says. "If you're faced with a problem, the first thing you do is, you ask people who have dealt with the problem before or who know how to do that kind of research, who can point you in the right direction." She drew in what she needed when she needed it, and kept the organization lean and mission-centric.

Although Heyman made all the decisions, they were all in service to the notion she started with, of taking the Israeli model and applying it to Rwanda. "My thinking was, here's an idea that I have," she says. "Now, is it a good idea? Is it going to work? Let's see if there is some methodology out there that I can follow and adapt." A tour of Israeli youth villages revealed that there were none she could straight-out copy, but she did find some that were loosely adaptable. From there, it was a matter of filling out the picture. In a town called Rubona in the eastern part of tiny Rwanda, she found some serviceable land near a major road, with access to electrical power. She located contractors as one would in the United States—by asking around, interviewing possible candidates, seeing work samples, choosing finalists, and making a selection. Then there was the money. Anne and her husband, Seth Merrin, a wealthy entrepreneur who created a wildly successful institutional trading service called Liquidnet, had established a family foundation that provided the initial funding for the venture and allowed Anne to focus exclusively on the work. Likewise, the American Jewish Joint Distribution Committee, which provides aid to needy individuals around the world, donated office space and "back office" support, such as accounting and oversight. But as the project advanced, Heyman felt obliged to turn for funding to other private individuals.

As she approached potential sources, though, she asked not just for money but for advice about how to proceed in a way that would increase the chances of securing funding. The answer came back: build it and they will come. In other words, find a way to get the project going, so that potential donors have something to see, and you can show that this village is no fantasy. The village itself and its residents would be indisputable proof of her intentions—and her abilities to deliver.

She gave herself a year to get the construction started. In Rwanda, that would be like making the deadline next week. "When I told the architect and builder that I wanted to do that, they almost fell on the floor." But it happened. It was actually less than a year later, in August of 2007, that the project broke ground in Rwanda.

By December of that year, 125 children had moved in, and, although only half the complex was built, they could start their schooling in one of the six finished classrooms. Agahozo-Shalom Youth Village was up and running. It looked like a true village, with a cluster of houses on the plain nearest the road; a community center up the hill, where someday there will be a library and a chapel; and a soccer field on the flat land adjoining. The school is on the hilltop so that the students can both see and be seen from a great distance. The school is its own advertisement.

"That was always the timeline," Heyman says matter-of-factly. "I was in a rush."

As the work progressed, so did Heyman's involvement. In those early months, she would typically spend ten days in Israel showing the Rwandans important aspects of the youth villages, ten days home in New York, and then ten days in Rwanda where she might be hunting for land while gathering a Rwandan advisory board to create a local commitment to her project.

And the toll on her family? She agonized about the sacrifice she was making as a parent—and that her three children were making in return. "But you know what?" she asks brightly. "I have never heard a word of complaint from any of them, not one, not even a heartbeat of one."

Some years into the project, Heyman got a call from her oldest son, Jason, who had gone to the village to make a publicity film for the village's annual Stand Up and Be Counted fundraiser in Manhattan. Initially, he had been concerned that the whole project

55

was a lot of money to spend on relatively few kids, and he had listened dubiously when his mother tried to tell him about "ripple effects" and how these kids were going to change the world. Now he got it. He'd just spent the day out in the fields with the kids from the village, all of them doing Tikkun Olam, Hebrew for repairing the world and widely interpreted as the pursuit of social justice. "You're right!" he shouted into the receiver. "It's happening. These kids aren't waiting until they graduate! They can't wait to go out and change the world. They're going to do unbelievable things."

As the creation of the village became more complex—adding the educational component, a small farm, a soccer program, and more—Heyman found the need to scale up the organization. There was too much for her to manage. So, reluctantly, she took on staff—she hired an executive director, a database manager, and someone to run the volunteer programs in New York. "If I'm needed for anything, I'm asked," she says. "But more and more they deal with the daily operations of the organization."

Inevitably, there have been gaps between the dream and the reality. She had intended to "build green," exclusively with renewable resources. This was largely a necessity, because there was no water or electricity on the land. She had wanted eventually to use solar power and wind turbines, and to sell that power back to the grid. It turned out that the economics involved in such sales were prohibitive—"they make no sense on any level"—but she was able to secure some solar technology through a donation from a U.S. company, and went ahead anyway. "Basically we said, you know what, let's just get on the electric grid. It's expensive, but we'll deal with that later." Meanwhile, she has assembled a team of engineering students from the United States to perform a village energy audit to see how much energy consumption could be cut, whether it made more sense to go with solar or wind for renewable energy, and how to educate the resident children about such topics. "So you throw the balls in the air," says Heyman, "and some of them you have to let drop, some you grab, and some you hand over to others."

For all of Heyman's entrepreneurial zeal, she has, almost uniquely in our sample, had the benefit of financial resources that are certainly not available to all social entrepreneurs. Her family's funding has freed her to concentrate on the task at hand in the early stages, so she didn't have to open up a second front, as it were—namely, the money quest that can often be a job all of its own. And she had key connections in the world of Jewish philanthropy that advanced the cause by providing her infrastructural help and also the contacts in Israel where she could hunt for a model for what she was attempting in Rwanda.

Such money and connections can be available to all social entrepreneurs, but usually at one remove, as they must find others willing to open a wallet or a Rolodex. Heyman's ability to tap immediately into both served as an accelerant and helped her concentrate exclusively on the work so that she could build her village at almost unimaginable speed. (But then, Heyman is an extraordinarily determined person, even by entrepreneurial standards.) For our purposes, her story shows how helpful, if not indispensible, money and connections can be. The more quickly these elements can be acquired, the faster the project can be realized.

It is one thing to have a brilliant idea, and quite another to actually bring it to life. Indeed, one might argue that it isn't truly a brilliant idea until it *has* been brought to life. In nonprofits as in everything else in life, it is all about the execution. To do good, you really have to be able to do it.

Rebecca Onie: No Money, No Problem

Heyman had the marked advantage of her family's funding to get started, but as we've already mentioned, that is a rarity in the nonprofit world. It is almost impossible to overstate how much easier it is to start a nonprofit if you have serious capital. It means that your entire focus can be on the work. (Of course, you may not be quite so rigorous in your analysis of some of your spending decisions.) Still, without such financial advantages, as a budding social entrepreneur you will have to rely on your ingenuity.

Take Rebecca Onie, who was just a Harvard sophomore when she started on her Project HEALTH, renamed Health Leads in 2010. She had no money, no connections—nothing except her obvious intelligence and an eagerness to help the poor. Thinking she would ultimately go into the law, she had done an internship investigating housing issues for Greater Boston Legal Services, where she met a "really inspiring crazy lawyer" named Jeff Purcell. Impressed with her initiative and savvy, Purcell put Onie out in the field where she could learn firsthand from low-income families about their housing needs. Inevitably the topic shifted from housing to medical care. For time and again, that was the real problem. The client who was about to be evicted because of a failure to pay rent? He was HIV-positive—and couldn't afford to pay for both his rent and his medication. And it went the other way too, from medical needs to housing problems. The child with asthma? She was living with her family in an apartment crawling with cockroaches, which can cause respiratory problems. The key factors in these supposed housing issues weren't just housing; they were a combination of health and poverty. Unfortunately, though, by the time Onie got involved, her clients were already in crisis.

She needed to take what she calls "a more preventive approach." She saw what such an approach might be when she happened to read a magazine article about Barry Zuckerman, the visionary chair of pediatrics at Boston City Hospital. He'd been trying to expand the standard definition of medical treatment to include all the services that would help make a child healthy. Not just surgery or pills, but grief counseling, nutrition advice, legal aid, and financial support. Onie called him, and pointed out that college students like herself might help him realize his ambitions. Zuckerman replied by inviting Onie to spend six months observing the work of a variety of pediatricians at Boston City Hospital and then drawing her own conclusions about what should be done. This she did, but she kept asking the doctors what they would prescribe for their patients if they had unlimited resources. They rarely said they'd suggest more medical treatment. Instead they recommended support—support of all sorts: legal, financial, psychological. For these, most believed, were the keys to their health.

It was just what she'd thought—and now the doctors were confirming it. Says Onie, "A kid has an ear infection or an asthma exacerbation, and the doctor prescribes antibiotics or an inhaler, but the kid doesn't get better. Why? Not for any medical reason. It's because he's living in a car, or his family has no food to eat."

And then it came to her: she would work toward expanding the definition of medical care for the poor by connecting families with the services they need to be healthy. She took this idea back to Purcell, and told him that she wanted to bring in other students and make this her work at the Boston Medical Center. "I was quite nervous to share this with him," she recalls. "He was this vigorous advocate for families with really high standards, and I was afraid he'd look down on me for wanting to engage my fellow undergraduates in doing this." But instead he told her, "You have a vision, and you have an obligation to realize that vision."

That was when she knew that she had to follow this through, wherever it might lead. It just felt right; it had that sense of fit that so many social entrepreneurs speak of. "Actually, it felt more right than any of my classes or other extracurriculars," she says. "It felt purposeful, like it made me most myself."

But this was also her check-in moment, a moment that all social entrepreneurs speak of, when she had to ask herself if she had what it took. If she were to act on Purcell's observation, she would be embarking on a course she was not yet prepared for. Unlike Heyman, Onie was just nineteen, still in college, penniless, and completely alone with her big plans.

But there are other resources besides financial ones. The trick is to be able to identify them. And this is what Onie did next. For her insight did not come in a single burst. It was more like fireworks, one colorful explosion leading to another.

Onie realized she did have unique access to a tremendously valuable resource that would help her realize her goal. Further, it was one that was immensely useful, adaptable, all-purpose, committed, energetic, available, and, best of all, free. It was the small army of college volunteers whom Onie was confident she could mobilize for this new endeavor. "Right then, in Boston, there were 114,000 college students," she says. "It was this huge untapped workforce. I kept thinking, there must be a way to make it the solution."

And of course there was, just by putting out the word. Volunteers are the life force behind nonprofits; it is the rare nonprofit that does not rely heavily on them. Most likely, that will be true of yours, too. Volunteers can be difficult to manage without money to reward performance, and they will need training, but they are free, and they are usually dedicated and eager to help. A common problem for volunteers, however, is to get them to value work for which they are not being compensated. It is always tempting to blow it off if something better comes along.

This was the problem Onie faced when she tried to enlist her first volunteer recruits at Harvard. They didn't take it seriously, and

Onie quickly figured out why. She saw that volunteer organizations at Harvard tended to set their expectations too low—and then seemed surprised that their student volunteers responded by doing the same. It came to her when she noticed that posters advertising for volunteers invariably made the work sound easy, convenient, and unchallenging. A snap! We'll take anybody! By contrast, the posters for varsity sports teams made the recruitment process look like a tour through hell. "They say it's going to be this hugely competitive process; you'll probably get cut; the practices are five days a week, take hours and hours, and start at six in the morning on some cruddy field across the river where you'll freeze your ass off," she says with a laugh. They don't even bother to mention the good part: that if you make the squad, you'll not only enjoy playing a sport you love but also probably find a community of lifelong friends, and you might even learn leadership skills that will make you CEO of a Fortune 500 company by age forty. Even so, students flocked to the sports tryouts and killed themselves to make the team.

So Onie turned that around. Following the varsity sports model, she made the volunteer work sound grueling—long hours, hard work, lengthy training, and cuts. "If volunteers don't perform or don't show up, we'll kick them out," she says now. The application process involved lengthy essays and a series of interviews.

It was brilliant. Harvardians rose to the challenge. Applications increased so much that Onie couldn't take more than a third of them. The winners agreed to commit for a full year, put in six hours a week (half in the clinic and half doing follow-up with families), and subject themselves to reviews that would help identify the non-performers. The harder Onie made it, the more the students liked it. And the more seriously Onie took it, the better the students did.

There was more, of course. Onie had to worry about fitting these student volunteers into the rather delicate ecosystem. She had to develop a parallel system of prescription pads that covered these nonmedical services, and, of course, she had to work out a way to match the needs with providers in the local community or from government agencies.

For all of this, Onie had to feel her way along. The notion of using college students to meet the extramedical needs of poor people sounded right, but would the students share her ambitions and act on them? Would the system respond? Like Heyman, she proceeded step-by-step. "We made no promises to anyone," she says. To the students, the hospital, or the families, she means. Then she grins. "The downside was that we were just a bunch of students, and it was hard to get it all going." She pauses. "The upside was that nobody actually expected us to succeed." And when they did? "I think it was truly surprising to people."

You could say that Onie's secret ingredient was her student volunteers, but it wasn't really. It was her ingenuity, both in identifying what she needed and in determining how to obtain it. It's a big world, and the answer is always out there somewhere. The trick is to ask the right questions to find it.

Relying on Your Internal Resources

Different as Heyman and Onie are in background and circumstances, they bear some important similarities, those that saw them through the many difficulties posed by their two very different start-ups, and those that are instructive about the character of successful social entrepreneurs generally. First and most important, neither of them ever met a challenge they didn't like. They thrived on difficulty, viewing it not as difficulty at all but as an opportunity to demonstrate their resourcefulness. This sends an important message out to the world, but also to the rest of the organization, and shows once more how much a nonprofit depends on its founder for inspiration, energy, determination, and character. A leader's external resources are useful, no question, but her *internal* resources are an essential part of what it takes to get a nonprofit organization off the ground; it is those qualities that will enable her and her organization to overcome the many challenges that life will inevitably throw her way.

CHAPTER 4

Getting off the Ground

At Some Point You Need to Get Real

LET'S ASSUME THAT YOU NOW have an idea for a nonprofit—an idea that grabs you, expresses you—and you've decided that you have what it takes to get this thing up and running. Now you're wondering how to make something of it.

Getting off the ground isn't easy. All ideas are abstract. Beautiful and inspiring as they may be, ideas aren't real until they come into the world and start doing things. Like Heyman's plans for a Rwandan youth village, Onie's nonmedical prescriptions, or any of the other brilliant notions of our social entrepreneurs, the ideas of any nonprofit are literally nothing until they become a reality. And that requires crossing a vast divide, moving from Just You to the engagement of others, fundraising, securing a place of operation, establishing procedures as the mission is identified and then acted on. Along the way, everyone will say that he or she has every confidence in you, but the truth is that hardly anyone genuinely expects you to succeed. This is what Rebecca Onie meant when she said that people found it "surprising" when her idea actually worked.

Every stage of the prelaunch phase is intended to inch the project closer to the big moment when your grand concept is tested in real time with real people. If you're smart, you won't do the reality check just once but repeatedly, at every stage of the project's evolution. It's like navigating a new route through unfamiliar territory—you're constantly checking to see where you are in relation to where you thought you were and to where you are going. And you draw information from all sources, not just from landmarks and road signs, but also from maps and a GPS. You probably don't do these things just once, but over and over, constantly comparing your idea of reality to reality itself. Social entrepreneurs need to do the same. You can't just trust your instincts or your luck.

Unlike most professionals, a social entrepreneur like you probably comes to your new ambition in life with little training, so you're always having to check to make sure you are on course. You're probably consulting your friends and asking, Is this a good idea? Are you interested in helping out? Do you know anyone else who might be? It would be smart to reach out to others who have done similar things or have useful expertise. Ideally, you'll cast your net widely, pulling in people with a variety of skills, attitudes, and backgrounds. As a rule, the more established the potential adviser, the more specific should be the advice you seek. Don't just ask, "What do you think of my idea?" Ask instead, for example, "What is the best approach to fundraising for a venture like this?" As the idea is shaped, both by your own impulses and by the responses of others, you would do well to start identifying the essential principles of your operation, starting with the why and the how, and writing them down. They'll be general at first, but in time they will make an important statement about what kind of organization yours is meant to be.

Tommy Clark: Making It Up One Step at a Time

In formulating his idea for Grassroot Soccer, an educational program that harnesses the positive influence of soccer to inspire and mobilize communities to stop the spread of HIV, Tommy

Clark circulated a five-page summary of the concept to soccer friends from Zimbabwe, and then persuaded three of those who were most taken by the idea—Ethan Zohn, Kirk Friedrich, and Methembe Ndlovu—to come to his house in Albuquerque and sit around his kitchen table to hash the thing out. There, over the weekend, they formulated a game plan to bring their idea into being, starting with becoming a 501(c)(3), which is the tax-exempt status granted by the IRS for qualifying nonprofit organizations and is often a requirement when applying for grants.

The notion of becoming a 501(c)(3) was suggested by Friedrich's mother, who worked in nonprofits. "And we all sort of said, 'What's that?' And, 'How do you do that?'" Clark recalls. "And we just made a list of things that we had to do." Or, rather, what they imagined they had to do. "So that was the short of it."

At that point, Clark scarcely knew the word "nonprofit," and had no particular plans to start one. He just wanted to use his soccer connections to help with the AIDS/HIV epidemic in Africa. That was what he focused on when he made his to-do list. "We were just thinking about this idea, and we all just wanted to kind of get going on it. So it was all about, Where do we go? What do we do? How do we do this? All that kind of thing. And then we made a big checklist, and tried to figure out who could handle what." One of the pieces was the 501(c)(3), which led to the first complication, as that nonprofit status requires a proper board of directors for the fledgling venture; this imposed a burden all its own. Who'd be good? Who would do it? We'll get into this whole thorny area in a later chapter, but Clark simply reached for the first competent people who would say yes. Told he needed a lawyer for the board, he enlisted his father-in-law. Told he needed a money man, he asked a CPA he knew, Jason Hix. Told that someone in the field of public health would be handy, he asked a family friend named Bill Wiese and, because Wiese served on other boards, made him board chairman.

Then they needed to field-test the notion. Would teachers even let a bunch of soccer players come into the schools to offer what amounted to a freeform class in sex ed? Would students go for it themselves? Would the professional soccer players want to get involved? Those were all essential questions that needed to be resolved before they could hope to set up an organization to promote such ideas.

It often seems that the key moment in the development of a nonprofit comes out of the blue, and it takes some time to register its significance. With Grassroot Soccer, curiously enough it wasn't anything anyone said. It was the way everyone spoke, the eager and happy intensity of their clamor to be heard. This was in Zimbabwe, where Clark had gone with his colleagues Friedrich and Ndlovu to recruit soccer players for the cause. They were able to win over a handful fairly quickly, and they decided to put them on display at a big dinner where Clark had invited several local headmasters and prominent teachers for a meal of grilled meat and a local cornmeal dish called sadza.

Dinner in Zimbabwe is customarily eaten in silence, the better for everyone to concentrate on the meal. It was so quiet, in fact, that Clark was concerned that it conveyed a lack of interest, if not downright hostility. "Nobody was talking," Clark says. When the meal was over, Clark gathered everyone together so he could tell the group about his plans for Grassroot Soccer. "Again, it was pretty quiet. I was worried that nobody was even going to talk about this." But then a few people piped up, and then a few more. "And pretty soon the conversation really got going. It turned out that people had a lot to say once they were given permission to say it." What made all the difference was the idea, the founding idea that Clark had started with, that soccer players could help curb the spread of HIV/AIDS. "It was definitely the idea," Clark agrees. "All of them—soccer players, teachers, students—had lost friends, brothers, sisters, girlfriends, boyfriends, husbands, wives, nieces, nephews. This was a chance for them to do something about that. I think that was the thing." So the essential building blocks of the new venture were in place. "We came back from that trip thinking that, yeah, the soccer players were on board, and the teachers, too. They thought it was important. We had the community."

Now they needed to come up with the money to make it all possible. For that, Clark dipped once more into his Rolodex and came up with Andrew Shue, who had played soccer with him at Dartmouth. The brother of the film actress Elisabeth Shue, Andrew was an actor on the hit TV show *Melrose Place*. He had started a nonprofit of his own, Do Something, so Clark figured he knew something about raising money. He was following the time-honored advice: try your family and friends first. So Clark turned to his in-laws in Boston, who held a party for the project and raised a few thousand dollars. That led to other, similar parties, which proved to be the organization's sole revenue source for the next two-and-a-half years. Clark kept his expenses down. All staffers were volunteers. He paid the team in Zimbabwe and the consultants who were developing the curriculum. "It seemed like a lot of money at the time," Clark says of the consultant fees, "but it was a really good move." The curriculum was the foundation of everything they did. He would pay other consultants to evaluate the curriculum later, once it was in use. He doesn't regret that expenditure either, for the same reason.

It was slow going, but he always felt the progress. "There was never a moment when we were thinking go–no-go, and thought no-go. It was always go." He pauses. "It was just, we just didn't know how to go or exactly what to do. So it was, how do we do it? We were all making this up as we went and trying to make it work. And the truth is, we're *still* trying to make sense of what we're doing and identifying the things that work well and the things that don't, and trying to do more of the things that work well. That was true then. And it's true now." Scientists sometimes speak of a phase change by which a solid changes into a liquid and then into a gas, as ice goes to water to water vapor. Something similar happens in nonprofits, too, as they go from being nothing to something. Clark could literally hear it happen as the conversation burst forth so excitedly around the table in Zimbabwe. The point of a step-by-step development of an idea isn't to grow it incrementally, but to grow it to the point at which it changes form, as water does when it turns to steam. This is the point where the idea becomes an organization.

Linda Fondren: Getting Organized

Linda Fondren is the founder of Shape Up Vicksburg and Shape Up Sisters, organizations dedicated to reducing obesity in her native Vicksburg, where, as in all of Mississippi, the obesity rate leads the nation, with a staggering 66 percent of the population classified as overweight or obese.

Fondren's sister was obese when she died of brain cancer. To Fondren, the obesity itself wasn't the issue. It was the consequences of the obesity—the fact that it kept her sister from enjoying her life. Fondren recalled that as her sister lay dying, she would say things like, "I wish I had lived my life more for myself." By that she meant that she had not been active, not engaged, not happy. Fondren was determined that other women in Vicksburg not share the same fate.

A real estate developer, Fondren started looking into gym franchises in which to place her exercise programs for overweight women. When she ran across a chain called Shape Up Sisters, the name leaped out at her. Enthralled, she bought the entire company and sold off the franchises outside Mississippi. She turned the remainder into gyms with programs that specialized in addressing the needs of overweight women. They had to, for such women are not likely to attend regular gyms. "They're too embarrassed," Fondren explains. "These are women who lack self-esteem, lack confidence, and just fitting into seats are struggles for them. But I believe *you must move*. Exercise is the key."

And how to get them moving? "Social connections," she says. "The gym has to offer a chance for them to connect with like kind, to have a conversation. And they don't even quite realize that they get healthy in the process." To find out just how healthy, she offered measures, too, an easy way of determining their body "composition"—the quantity of muscle and fat, the body mass index, the water content.

That desire for social connection led Fondren to think in terms of the wider community as well, because she believed that it would take a general sense of support for these overweight women to get moving again. She started to mobilize that support from the various elected officials in Vicksburg, from hospitals and doctors, restaurants, businesses. "I asked everyone to come together as a community so that we can help each other, and everyone was more than happy to come on board. I didn't get one no." And the idea of getting people moving spread out from the gym to the streets, where Fondren organized walking clubs along the brick-paved streets of Vicksburg. She persuaded restaurants to offer healthier menus, hospitals to provide free cholesterol readings and diabetes checks. Finally she offered a challenge to all of Vicksburg: shed seventeen thousand pounds in seventeen weeks. It wasn't much, if you worked out the figures—only a half-pound per person. The city didn't meet that initial goal, but still, Fondren was not disheartened. She kept at it, and Vicksburg residents lost over fifteen thousand pounds in one year. That accomplishment was enough to draw the attention of CNN, which saluted Fondren on air as one of its Top 10 Heroes of 2010.

Creating Structure: The Six Keys to Success

The life course of Fondren's nonprofit as it moved from inception to becoming established reads like an inevitable progression from one thing to the next, but the particular flow of these events was not inevitable. Instead, it was the result of myriad strategic decisions that Fondren made, many of them so intuitively that she was scarcely aware of making them at all. But, in every case, progress is the result of strategy, even as it dictates strategy. What was Fondren trying to do? Improve lives by reducing weight. How? By making it a community effort. To what end? To lose seventeen thousand pounds in seventeen weeks. Every level of strategic decision leads to, and from, another level.

Students of business have discerned essential elements to strategic plans like the one that Fondren carried in her head. They are as follows:

1. A defined *mission* that identifies the core purpose of the organization
2. A more precise *goal* that transforms the mission into something doable
3. A clear *objective* that is more achievable and near term
4. A *strategy* to accomplish that objective
5. The *actions* required to execute the strategy
6. The *measurement* of results that will reveal success

These elements have some of the quality of a battle plan, because they involve seizing opportunities much as armies seize territories. Whether the planner employs them consciously or not, they define the planning structure for most nonprofits, and for for-profits, too, for that matter. They help an organization's leaders decide what to do next. Fondren didn't follow this rubric consciously, acknowledging that she didn't think strategically "right off the bat." Instead, like most nonprofit founders, she started with a "vision or a passion" and went from there.

Fair enough, but it still helps to lay out the process of determining *where* the organization might go from there. For Fondren, what she calls vision or passion might better be termed *mission,* which is, as she says, where everything starts. A mission is a quick summation of the organization's reason for being, its purpose in life. For Fondren, Shape Up Vicksburg was all about giving obese and overweight residents of Vicksburg a fresh start.

Because a mission serves as the all-important handle on an organization, it is best if it's inspiring. The mission of Jordan Kassalow's VisionSpring, for instance, would not be spreading glasses through the developing world, although that is the bare truth of the matter. It might be better described as transforming lives with clearer vision. Wording the mission that way gives the organization more lift. Carolyn LeCroy's Messages Project isn't so much to help prisoners by sending home messages by video as it is to keep their families together. And so Fondren's mission might be described as giving obese and overweight Vicksburg residents a new chance at life.

Such a statement sets down a marker that declares what the organization is all about. It does this and only this. It is a fixed point on the landscape. There are many descriptions of organizational planning models, but one we especially like is that of the business analyst Thomas Wolf, who in his book *Managing a Nonprofit Organization in the Twenty-First Century* refers to management as a "journey." By this standard, the mission reveals, he says, "why the organization is making the journey."[1] Where it is going—that's a matter of goals, which determine the organization's direction to a particular area of need. For Fondren, whereas her mission might be giving obese and overweight women a new chance at life, the goal addresses how she plans to achieve that mission, how she would help obese and overweight women lose weight. In referring to the level below that, Wolf speaks of narrower objectives and targets, which show the precise destination—the street address, if you will—that the organization is trying to reach. For Fondren this might be the particular weight loss objective, those seventeen thousand pounds. Beyond that, Wolf introduces the concept of *strategies,* which act as the map showing how the organization can reach its objectives. For Shape Up Vicksburg, this might be the various in-gym weigh-ins, the revised restaurant menus, the hospital testing. Next come actions, or actually taking the trip, by which Wolf means doing the work of the organization in accordance with the plans already laid out, and seeing how it goes. Finally, Wolf then looks at one last level, evaluation, the measurements that we will take up in more detail later on in the book. This is a way of checking to see if the organization really is moving toward its destination. For Fondren, evaluation is a matter of measuring, by scales and other means, whether the women in her target group are indeed getting slimmer, more fit, and more engaged with life. After all, there can be no success without measurement.

When you address all these levels of planning, you will have created a structure for success and be well on your way to getting off the ground.

Learning as You Go

In the course of assembling a nonprofit, you may try to be methodical by making what amounts to a to-do list and checking off each task when it's done, as if starting a nonprofit were like packing for a trip or shopping for groceries. This makes sense, but you should be aware that you may not know what you need; that what you seek may not be on the shelf and, even if it is, can be difficult to find; and that once you find it, you may discover that it isn't quite right.

The basic problem is that you don't know what you don't know. All you know is that you have a burning desire to do something that has never been done before by anyone. Remember, things won't always go according to plan. You'll make plenty of mistakes—count on it. The important thing is to learn from them. Don't waste the chance! There is no one moment of creation, but thousands, and most of them in response to some mistake or other. But in order to learn from your mistakes, you need to get started—so that you can start making them.

CHAPTER 5

Being the Brand

Identifying with Your Organization

IT MAKES SENSE THAT NONPROFITS SHOULD, oftentimes, be very rooted in a person's life. As with the best for-profit companies, nonprofits are extremely personal statements of value and philosophy. Their creators say, *I believe this is vitally important, not just for me but for the world, so much so that I am going to devote all my energy, imagination, talent, and social connections to it*. And, given such a passionate involvement, you, as the founder of your own nonprofit, will become deeply identified with it as well. You will become the physical embodiment of the organization, its brand, far more than a for-profit CEO who is likely to be with the company only for a short hitch before pushing on to a new opportunity. After thirty years, Geoffrey Canada, the president and CEO of the Harlem Children's Zone, is now so iconic that he appears in American Express ads. He *is* that organization. Likewise, Anne Heyman, the dynamic creator of the Agahozo-Shalom Youth Village for Rwandan orphans, looms over that endeavor like the sky.

Such tight identification of creator to creation has its advantages, beyond the obvious one of a social entrepreneur demonstrating fierce loyalty to her cause. For one thing, it is most helpful in marketing, in getting the message out. The first order of business of any new nonprofit is, What is it? Who is it for? How does it work? Anything new is inherently inchoate, difficult to visualize and hard to describe. It makes it much easier if there is a face to which one can attach this vision. Your face helps make it real, and to the extent that your own life experience reflects the mission, that will make it more real still. This can be burdensome if you are already besieged by the many obligations of your start-up. David Suzuki, the host of a long-running nature show on Canadian television, was most reluctant to lend his name to a new environmental organization that he and his wife were founding. Because Suzuki was a national celebrity, the Al Gore of Canada, the organizers were eager to call the new entity the David Suzuki Foundation. His name would give it instant credibility and name recognition, as well as indicate the perspective of environmental activism that he is known for. But Suzuki was worried about being too closely identified with the project. "I argued long and hard about that, for I knew that if it carried my name, I could never walk away from it," he says, "no matter how old I was." He was also afraid that if he were the officially named founder, his opinion might carry more weight than it deserved.

In the end, the organization did indeed become the David Suzuki Foundation. But even if it hadn't, it would have been that implicitly. As a founder, you can't help being deeply identified with the nonprofit you start, for in a media-dominated age, it needs that identity. Ours is culture of personality. Unless your nonprofit is animated by your personality, it will be impersonal, even abstract. Look at the names of some of our eighteen nonprofits—the Genocide Intervention Network, STRIVE, Health Leads, City Year. All of them are right-sounding, and some may seem vaguely familiar, but only City Year has achieved anything close to the celebrity that generates images to go with the name. The Genocide Intervention Network has now done more to curb genocide than any other organization in the world, but it still needs Mark Hanis's remarkable background as a native of Ecuador who started the group as a Swarthmore junior for it to click with the public. Some of this blurriness is due to the fact that few nonprofits can afford a national advertising campaign or the heavy PR effort that draws free media coverage. Without a personal story to attach to, Michael Brown's trailblazing City Year would probably still be a mystery—the year of the city? A year in a city? But Brown's own long association with the cause of a domestic Peace Corps—first as a Harvard student pushing for a congressional bill on the subject with then Congressman Leon Panetta, and later working for Mayor Ed Koch, who started a demonstration project in New York City—both clarified and publicized the mission.

For-profits gain definition from their heavily advertised products, but nonprofits are forever in danger of remaining well-meaning abstractions, their do-good missions a kind of civil religion, one that lacks such key identifiers as a god, a church, a creed, or a congregation. But as the founder, you can provide the necessary lift to raise your organization into the limelight. Your story is the focal point, but so is your zest in putting that story forward. Stars are called stars for a reason. They have a luminescence and a loft that commands attention. You do, too. Even without movie credits, you are doing something good in the world, and that will turn heads. Let it.

Jay Feinberg: His Foundation Was His Life

When a nonprofit's mission is tied into the founder's identity, it lends stunning clarity and urgency to the cause. The best example of this is the Gift of Life Foundation, an organization for finding tissue donors, which grew out of the determination of a young foreign exchange analyst named Jay Feinberg and his parents, Jack and Arlene Feinberg, to find a donor whose bone marrow would cure Jay's potentially fatal leukemia. When Jay's immediate family offered no matches, his doctors feared that the cause was hopeless. Jay is an Ashkenazi Jew, which meant that his genetic inheritance would be virtually missing from bone marrow banks because so many of the Ashkenazi Jews were killed in the Holocaust. The doctors expected him to go home quietly and, Feinberg says, "wait for the inevitable." There in the doctor's office, Feinberg burst into tears, but he didn't give up hope.

Nor did his mother. "I don't think my doctor realized the power of the Jewish mother," Feinberg laughs. "If a doctor says, 'Don't worry, there are a lot of medications we can give your son when the time comes,' the Jewish mother is not likely to be too happy about that." Indeed, Jay's mother wasn't.

Feinberg's parents immediately set up shop in their living and dining rooms and, with unflagging energy, started cranking out makeshift fliers searching for potential donors for Jay. Each one had a paragraph of explanatory text with Jay's photo taped to the top. The Feinbergs then photocopied the whole thing and distributed it as widely as they could manage. Soon, as many as twenty volunteers a day pitched in to help them, working out of two thousand square feet of donated office space.

Then there was Feinberg himself. Rather than remain behind the scenes, he emerged front and center as the key focus of the campaign, the ultimate poster child. The brand image. He made this not just a matter of life or death, but of *his* life or death, and the public responded. "It wasn't rocket science," he says flatly. "It was really pretty simple: we knew that if we wanted people to turn out the numbers we needed, we'd have to tug at their heartstrings." It had to be personal.

In the end, sixty thousand potential donors were recruited, primarily in North America but also in Israel, a phenomenal accomplishment for a grassroots campaign by a family of three who were complete neophytes in a new and rapidly evolving medical field. "We achieved the numbers we did because it was an urgent appeal for Jay Feinberg, and here's his picture and here's a little bit of his story and his need," says Feinberg. "That's what motivated people. That's *still* what motivates people. The fact that there is a name and a face attached makes all the difference, and it's not just a generic drive."

Still, the generosity of the public floors him. "Nowadays, for something like this you'd do a cheek swab because of the DNA methodologies," he says. "But back then you'd have to draw blood, so we'd get thousands of people coming out in these blood drives for a total stranger, willing to stretch out their arms to save that person's life, someone they didn't know except by a picture and some words on a pamphlet, and may never have an opportunity to meet."

That person, of course, was Feinberg himself.

Feinberg, in his need, reached out to them, and they responded not just with blood but also with caring. As the slow, agonizing months of his search turned into years and reached past the three-year limit the doctors placed on his likely survival, Feinberg lived on ever more powerful chemotherapy and other heavy medication—and on the hope that these generous souls gave him. He says, "I have to say that while the whole experience might have been terrifying, that was really inspiring, and it is what really kept me going."

And, in the end, the effort paid off. By then, Feinberg had given up on finding a perfect match and had turned, reluctantly, to plan B—a bone marrow donor who was a match only minimally. It was a way of doing something, at least. By amazing fortune, though, in those last months, Feinberg had allowed other cancer patients in need of donors to join his search, and one of them, a college student from Toronto, had found a lifesaving match that way. Supremely grateful, the student and his close friend from Chicago were determined to return the favor by hosting a drive for Feinberg at a Yeshiva in Milwaukee. He was going to drive there with some friends, but one of them, a neighbor, couldn't go, and asked her sister to go instead. The sister was Becky Faibisoff. She hadn't intended to be tested because she was afraid of needles. She was going just to help out. But in the end, she summoned the courage and did it. She was the very last one of all the potential donors from the drive to be tested.

And Becky Faibisoff was the match.

When he got sick, Feinberg had been accepted at law school, and the school had held a place for him for the four years of his illness. Once he was well again, he wasn't so sure he wanted to attend after all. When the dean called to ask him about his plans, Feinberg said he should free the space for someone else. "I told him my life had taken another direction," Feinberg says. "It was really a no-brainer." He wanted to take what he had built for his own search and use it for others. It was always a nonprofit, but now it would be a nonprofit with a greater cause than just himself. It wouldn't be the Friends of Jay Feinberg anymore; it would be called the Gift of Life. It was intended to take advantage of the many innovations it had come up with—relying on the then-new Internet, amassing databases and testing techniques—that Jay had explored already in his own urgency.

But in making the organization less about him, Feinberg had to recalibrate his own role in difficult and unexpected ways as the Gift of Life shifted from being a family operation to a more institutional one. He remained at the vital center of it, though, not only as its CEO and the face of the organization but also as its reason for being, its founding myth. His story, after all, was *the* story.

Using Your Story

Even more than a for-profit company, any nonprofit you start will be a virtual organization, one that exists in the public mind far more as an idea than as a physical entity. Most likely, it will never have fancy headquarters, a vast manufacturing plant, or products shown on TV. But it can provide tangibles in other ways, chiefly as concepts, as ideas—to bring glasses to developing countries or help prisoners relate to their children. But even those missions aren't fully brought home unless your own story, as the creator, is woven into them, as we have just seen with Jay Feinberg. That example is extreme, because Feinberg was, at least initially, both the agent and the recipient of his cause. It was indeed all about him. But this is true for the other nonprofits more than you might imagine. You are the totem of your enterprise, the person who sums it all up. It is essential that you use your story, yourself, and your image to advance your cause. Doing so isn't self-centered; it is life centered, because it is using what you have to advance the cause that will make life better for others. It's an act of generosity.

CHAPTER 6

The Pros and Cons of Partnerships

Do Your Research

IT'S ONE THING TO COME UP with an exciting idea for a brand-new nonprofit; it's another to prove that you can really do it, and another still to establish that this project isn't already being done.

When Rebecca Onie finally cooked up the idea of deploying students to help the poor meet their extramedical needs, she had to ask the sensible question: Was there any other nonprofit already addressing this issue? If there was another organization going at it, was there any place for hers? In nonprofits no less than in the arts, originality is everything. No one wants to be part of a me-too enterprise.

These were essential questions, and Onie knew she couldn't rely on guesses and assumptions for the answers. In the course of her months at the hospital, talking to doctors and staff, Onie painstakingly investigated the needs of the low-income families in the neighborhoods near the Boston Medical Center and surveyed other providers to see whether those needs were already being met. She did this herself, by phone or in person. She discovered no competition. But if she had, she could have followed up by calling any of the organizations in question and asking them hard questions about what they did, and for whom.

This is where the social sector can differ from the private. This kind of organizational information sharing isn't considered to be inappropriate prying. It wasn't as if she were trying to dig up trade secrets. Nonprofits can reasonably be proprietary about some aspects of their operation, but not about their service area and the needs they meet. And, these days, the Internet and email make such queries seem less intrusive. They allow a stranger like Onie to introduce herself and present her questions, and her respondent to get back to her at his or her convenience, leaving a written record of the entire communication.

If an email you send leads to a phone conversation, here are some tips: don't talk too much, and don't overexplain: you're there to listen and learn. And pay attention to what the other person—preferably the executive director (ED)—is *not* saying just as closely as to what she is. If the ED says with some scorn that her organization would never get into something like what you are contemplating, press her to say why. Your idea may be a threat, and the ED is being defensive, or she could be telling you something important that you don't know. Don't accept the assumption that such a venture is simply not to be considered. Gently press her to give her reasons and then evaluate them for yourself.

Just because something has not been done doesn't mean it shouldn't be. Then again, if it has been tried but the effort has failed, that's important to know. Find out what went wrong. A few tweaks to a failed endeavor might generate success; also, things change, and today's environment might be much more hospitable to your project. Innovative new companies like Facebook, Netflix, and countless others have emerged the way nonprofits need to—by seizing on current needs, technologies, and ideas to create something new and desirable.

The apparent lack of such services, of course, is what made Onie think along these lines in the first place, but subsequent inquiry only confirmed her initial impression. No one else was doing this. Just to be sure, she continued to survey the field as her idea for Project HEALTH began to take shape. Such outside validation can offer important assurances.

In the course of surveying the field of other organizations doing work in your area, you might come across one whose interests run so close to yours that you're tempted to abandon your effort altogether. That may prove to be the sensible course; there's no point reinventing the wheel. But think this through before you give up. Make sure that there really is too much overlap and, if there is, consider joining forces. There's no shame in that, and you might be able to increase the existing organization's reach and perspective. However, you might feel that the other organization's mission doesn't truly duplicate yours, that it encroaches just enough on your space to feel threatening. Knowing that it's well established and up and running while you are still trying to get yours going can initially be dispiriting, but it can lead to an enlivening result all the same.

Scott H. Silverman: The Benefits of Joining Forces

Scott H. Silverman, the man who created the rehabilitation program Second Chance, worried that his program was starting to flounder a few years after it was founded. He had been determined to start the operation on a businesslike basis, complete with a Dun & Bradstreet credit rating, one of the few quasi-public agencies to have one. He explains that Second Chance "has always been a business model for me. I think of myself as someone who is building human capital." The problem was, the business wasn't coming in. "I had a zero budget for almost four years," he says. "No money." It took him four years to land his first donor. Critics complained that Silverman was relying too much on the inspiration of his personal story, his remarkable charisma, and too little on a systematic program that could run without him. "Everyone said, you don't have a program. I said, well, I'm meeting with people one-on-one, coaching them through the interview process, helping them get a job. But, they said, you need a program; otherwise you can't get funding."

In one of the serendipitous moments that seem to govern Silverman's career, he happened to see an episode of *60 Minutes* about a program started in Harlem called STRIVE that did much of what Silverman was attempting to do, but did it better. Instead of feeling threatened, Silverman considered it a godsend. "So I saw this thing on TV, and I'm like, my God! Here's a curriculum! If I could only get this out to San Diego. And that was instrumental in helping the exponential growth of the organization." He struck a deal with STRIVE, the organization run by former convict Robert Carmona (whom we met briefly in Chapter Two). STRIVE became the software for Silverman's hardware. It delivered the educational message of Second Chance. "STRIVE helped invigorate, reinvigorate me," he says. And it gave Second Chance a second chance, allowing Silverman to think not just one at a time, but twenty, thirty at a time. "We could finally build capacity," he says. "What I'm thinking about now is what would happen if we could impact one hundred a month, twelve hundred a year. What could we do then?"

A number of the entrepreneurs from our sample ended up relying on larger host organizations; and, as a neophyte, you might also, because existing organizations often have much of what you need to acquire—chiefly experience, security, and stability. They have a public identity that can give you, as a new social entrepreneur, a sense of legitimacy. And, of course, most important of all, if they are established going concerns, they have funding, and if your mission meshes with theirs and they find it beneficial to take you under their wing, they might provide you some of it, either in cash or in kind.

Sara M. Green: Getting Up and Running with a Host Organization

Sara M. Green of Art for Refugees in Transition (ART) was lucky enough to find a larger organization to help with her plan to bring art to refugees. She had gone to business school to learn how to handle her nonprofit, and her nonprofit professor encouraged her to write up a business plan laying out her idea and describing the potential market and funding sources. As part of her plan, she performed the usual due diligence to determine if any other organization was doing this kind of work, and she discovered, to her relief, that the answer was no. But she wasn't sure how her nonprofit would survive on its own, either. It was hard enough to raise funds for domestic arts programs; she feared it would be nearly impossible to find donors for foreign ones, involving refugees no less. Without such donations, she couldn't afford the airfare, let alone the necessary infrastructure expense to establish a presence in a refugee camp miles from anywhere, as her plan entailed.

"So my professor encouraged me to partner up," she says. He recommended a connection he had at UNICEF, which proved to be unreceptive, as did Save the Children, which she tried next. By a quirk, the president of the International Rescue Committee (IRC) was also teaching in Green's nonprofit course. The IRC had been in operation since the close of World War Two and had outposts in many refugee camps in Africa, Asia, and Europe. The president was intrigued, and passed Green on to the head of a department called Children in Armed Conflict. "I met with her, presented our idea, and she said, 'Wow! This is fabulous! Nobody's doing this.'" Bingo. The department head offered to bring Green's ART into partnership with their community development programs. Unable to offer a program like Green's on its own, it welcomed her project into the IRC fold. And, better still, it offered to help raise money for her program and to implement it overseas, starting with a program for Burmese refugees in Northern Thailand and continuing to other spots under the auspices of other organizations.

The IRC graciously welcomed Green into two camps in Thailand, providing her entrée there, and a base for her operations, neither of which she could have acquired on her own. "There's no way to get into a refugee camp unless you are already registered," she concedes.

> You can't just walk in and say, "Knock, knock. I'm here. I want to do good." It doesn't really work that way. I knew that if I had to sit down and do the financials for this, if I had to raise money for an interpreter, for a Jeep, for somebody on the ground, a runner to get me camp passes, to have enough money to bribe the people to give them to me, because they don't know who I am—to build all of that basic infrastructure, that's ridiculous. Nobody's going to give that money to me. Who am I?

The merging of the two entities, one large and established, the other small and untried, has not gone smoothly. There have been the usual assortment of bureaucratic tussles, ego clashes, and communication breakdowns, but in the end, the IRC did deliver, and without its help, Green's program would have stopped before it even got started.

Darell Hammond: The Promise and Peril of Partnership

When you link up with another organization, you have many options as to how to go about it. A partnership? A program of the host organization? A division? A department? As a general rule, you probably want to retain as much autonomy and control over the destiny of your organization as possible, but you have to face reality, too.

Darell Hammond confronted this problem when he was starting KaBOOM!, the playground-building operation. The problem, of course, was money. The agency was getting money, but it always came with strings attached. A backer of the playground project in a community might offer to kick in $70,000—but only if the build took place on Thursday in time for the backer's potluck. But the community itself was all set to build on Saturday and was arranging a community picnic to celebrate. Such wrangles led to disappointing compromises, and one party or the other would feel shortchanged. As Hammond reviewed the revenue options, he wondered about turning to corporations for funding. But he worried that he might be co-opted, turned into a piece of the corporate promotion budget, and end up sacrificing too much of what made KaBOOM! so meaningful. "It would be all about the corporation," he says, "and not about the community."

He realized that he didn't have to look at the funding issue as a toggle switch, where it would be all corporation or none, but rather as a dial, by which he could adjust the intensity of the corporate involvement to an acceptable point. The question was entirely academic until Hammond happened to participate in a panel discussion at the annual conference of the Enterprise Foundation in Miami. One of his fellow panelists was the head of community affairs for Home Depot, and, as Hammond said, "He took a liking to me." A strong liking, it turned out, one worth $200,000 that first year of their partnership. That in turn led to a $2.7 million investment from consumer products giant Kimberly-Clark. Later Ben & Jerry's came in, as did a Chicago insurance company called CNA. These relationships not only funded KaBOOM!'s activities but also gave the organization something Hammond had not thought to value—a corporate perspective. KaBOOM! has imported a fair amount of that perspective, as an unexpected benefit of these partnerships. KaBOOM!'s COO ran Ben & Jerry's for eight years—"a triple-bottom-line business," Hammond adds, referring to the multiple agendas of the company beyond profit maximization. Its CFO came from a $16 billion company. The head of marketing and communications performed the same role for Animal Planet. The head of development had previously done corporate development for Habitat for Humanity. Quite a roster. But these experienced executives demonstrate the essential complexity of the relationship. How deeply can KaBOOM! be enmeshed with business before it loses the freshness of an identity that is reflected in the colorful, jokey halls of the company's offices outside Washington, or at a community build? "Many people have actually thought we've been a division of Home Depot," Hammond says. "They get so much recognition and credit that it's almost like 'Powered by KaBOOM!' And to be honest, our proposition is that we're not about the credit, we're about the cause. And if that means we don't get the credit, so be it." The relationship between KaBOOM! and Home Depot shows the benefits and liabilities of a strategic partnership between a nonprofit and a commercial interest as it underscores the risks and benefits to both. After all, the purpose of the organization was never to build a playground but to build a community by building a playground. But no corporation is ever going to have much luck making people think that that community was brought to you by the corporation. Not in the context of a nonprofit where corporations will be perceived as visitors, never residents.

And so, while Hammond has earned Home Depot and his other corporate partners a great deal of good will, his organization has received from them something more essential—the funding to continue with the essential enterprise, free of the hassles of endless fundraising.

Partnerships: A Scorecard

Partnerships are nothing to be scorned. They are not sellouts or diminishments or shameful compromises. They are an important option in the life of a nonprofit, as they can provide ways to sustain a fledgling organization that otherwise might not grow, and possibly not survive. A potential partner should be viewed as a possible resource, one that has to be evaluated both in terms of what it can add and in terms of what it might subtract. As a founder, you will need to consider this carefully. Also keep in mind a question that too many founders have forgotten: Will you be happy in a structure where you are no longer the boss?

CHAPTER 7

Finding Support

Use Your Connections

NEEDLESS TO SAY, NO NONPROFIT RUNS on air. It is fueled by time and effort—and, of course, by money, which is always in short supply. And whereas for some nonprofits a partnership is a perfect solution to this problem, partnering up with another organization is not always ideal, sensible, or even possible. Organizations striking out on their own need to find other means of support, and unlike start-up for-profit companies, a nonprofit typically won't rely on a bank loan (except in the rarest of circumstances) because the nonprofit usually has no stream of revenue to generate the funds for payback. Venture capitalists won't give you a penny. But money is available all the same. It's all around you. You just have to know where to look.

One way to think of the likely targets is as an array of concentric circles with you at the epicenter. If you're like most social entrepreneurs, you won't have much in the way of assets, and you'll be a bit nervous about parting with what little you have. Instead, you'll turn first to your family, starting with your parents. After all, they have probably supported you in most of your ventures so far, many of them quite pricey (perhaps college tuition, the down payment for a house, a wedding). You might think your request will catch your family by surprise, but that is not likely. After all, you have doubtless been talking up your nonprofit idea and passion for months, if not years.

Aside from your parents, of course, you are likely to have plenty of other family members to choose from—siblings, uncles, remote cousins, and even those quasi-relatives that are longtime friends of the family, if you think they might care about your cause. Remember, though, to pitch the cause, not the connection. Although some kindhearted relatives might say yes regardless of how you frame the question, strategically it is wise to frame it in terms of your own passion and dedication for the cause, maybe even in terms of the enormous sacrifice you are making, whether that is giving up a much-loved job or putting aside your long-held plans for graduate school for a cause that is greater than yourself. Don't assume that just because someone is your relative, she is going to shower money on some whim of yours. If you are interested in creating a museum of the postage stamp, go to him only if he is a philatelist. This holds true for all but your own closest friends as well. Sad to say, but any bond between you improves the likelihood only that the potential donor will hear you out, not that he or she will write you a check. This is what makes working in nonprofits so hard.

The cardinal rule still holds. Do not view this as a chance for anyone to do a favor for you. View it as a chance for you to do a favor for her. Philanthropy is not altruism; it is much closer to narcissism. So when you make your pitch, think entirely of the benefits to the potential donor, the satisfaction and pleasure she will take in advancing a cause that is already close to her heart. Rest assured, that is what she is thinking of.

Never apologize for thinking in terms of personal connections. Access is key, for almost anyone with extra money is hidden behind secret addresses, unlisted cell numbers, and unavailable email addresses. One wealthy philanthropist we know has two sets of business cards in his wallet, one that includes his email address and one that does not. He determines which card to give out depending on whether he is willing to allow the receiver to get in touch with him later on. For a neophyte social entrepreneur, access to such a person is everything, for he can provide a great many of the necessities of the field—funding, connections, advice. So when you do have access to people who can help, don't be afraid to approach them. After all, just about every nonprofit needs to acquire recognition and money before it can come into existence.

Mark Hanis: Spreading the Word and Gaining Support

Mark Hanis was raised in Ecuador. As a young boy, he attended a private school that helped support the nearby community, whose residents made their livelihood mining through garbage. Through his school, Mark became actively engaged with the children of the homeless people in the community. As a student at Swarthmore, he taught a Bangladeshi cafeteria worker how to use email so that she could write home. Small as they were, these efforts were his only preparation for his campaign to stop the killing in Darfur, a project that soon grew into a global political campaign against genocide.

He was moved to undertake his campaign by Nicholas Kristof's columns in the *New York Times* on the appalling mass atrocities in Darfur. He was especially moved by one particular Kristof piece that told the story of a woman who had to decide which child to send out for the firewood she needed to cook their food. If she sent her son, he might be shot. If she sent her daughter, she might be gang-raped. Says Hanis, "To me, I don't find there's a lot to say after reading that except 'What can I do to help?'"

Even as a college kid, he was a pragmatist, and he knew better than to try to stop genocide by trying to stop genocide. He knew to go for something smaller, something winnable, something that could be leveraged. Reading further about Darfur, he discovered that there was a small army of African Union peacekeepers, a kind of UN force concentrated on the African continent, that was preparing to intervene, but it faced serious logistical shortfalls, such as a lack of tents, and it was without the money to address these needs. That was it: Hanis and his fellow classmates would set themselves the task of contributing money toward the tents and other logistical necessities.

"It was manageable," Hanis says. "Bite-sized." And that proved to be a hallmark of all his efforts to stop genocide. Genocide is such a massive issue that it can't be attacked head-on but only obliquely, with targeted efforts that are inevitably partial, but that can be a focus of effort and an inspiration for more. "That's how we think about engagement," he says. "We call it the three E's: easy, effective, and entertaining." In this, he was approaching the problem very much from his perspective as a busy college kid—a perspective that would be shared by his target audience, which was organized as a kind of youth brigade, and would work upward through the age ranks from there. Hanis believed that because everybody is oversubscribed already, altruism has to be easy. Otherwise people will shift their attention to something that is. Because nobody has much free time, the effort has to be short term but high impact. And—this was probably his most brilliant insight—to be enticing, participation in his cause had to be fun. You didn't do it because you should. You did it because you wanted to. Guilt was bad.

Having worked out the core principles, Hanis and his colleagues needed to shape the intellectual foundation for his organization, to let everyone know where he was coming from. For this, they relied on *A Problem from Hell: America and the Age of Genocide,* Samantha Power's Pulitzer Prize–winning book on genocide, which observed that the citizens of advanced nations have failed to stop genocide, not because they don't care, but because they haven't summoned the political will to succeed.[1] That inspired Hanis and his classmates to develop a persistent political constituency against genocide that would drive up the cost of politicians' ignoring the issue.

To learn how to do that, Hanis and his colleagues did a road tour down K Street, the corridor of lobbyists in Washington DC, and consulted some of the most effective political organizations, not just on the left, but all across the political spectrum: Focus on the Family and the NRA along with the Sierra Club and MoveOn. Hanis says the message from all of them was, "If you expect to take effective political action, you've got to have effective political advocates. It's not enough to have people wear wristbands. You have to get them to take effective political action. You have to train them." It was almost as if they needed to take a seminar in the political basics. Hanis ticks off the topics: "How does a bill become law? How do you write an op-ed? How do you fundraise? How do you organize?" He realized he needed a scorecard to record and publicize the degree of devotion of political leaders to the cause. To empower private citizens to push their representatives, Hanis and his team created an 800-number hotline (1-800-GENOCIDE) that, using the caller's ZIP Code, directs them to the offices of their congressman and senator, or to the White House, so they can cajole their elected leaders directly. And easily.

Hanis realized that, initially, the Darfur campaign would go in two directions, first toward raising money for the tents, but second toward generating publicity for the cause. Those two were in service to a third: influencing the Washington policymakers who, more than anyone else, held the future of Darfur in their hands.

To get anywhere with such a campaign, Hanis figured he'd need major publicity, and for that, it would help to secure the prominent backing of a boldfaced political name, and that meant an op-ed piece. In a wonderful example of the combination of innocence and cynicism that all nonprofits create eventually, Hanis and a classmate wrote a persuasive op-ed detailing the importance of the cause, and then set about to find a more impressive byline than their own to run it under.

This is where access can be so useful. As a twenty-year-old college kid, Hanis had none. But he did have time, chutzpah, and a fair degree of technological savvy. He managed to suss out the email addresses of thought leaders all over town, and sent plaintive emails asking the recipients if they would be willing to adopt the orphan op-ed he attached. On this basis, he succeeded in "coldmailing" quite a roster of heavyweights: Jimmy Carter, Henry Kissinger, and "just about any former secretary of state, former president, former people in the National Security Council." He got nowhere with any of them.

Hanis continued his emailing efforts with no luck, until—at last—success. He received an email from Gayle Smith, who had been President Clinton's senior director for African affairs. She wrote to say she'd been very impressed and moved by his op-ed. She wouldn't put her name to it, but she would do him one better: she'd "make it happen." She would do her best to broker a deal with the African Union troops.

That was certainly fine with Hanis and his colleagues. It still got them the support they needed. At the end of 2004, Smith flew to Africa to meet with representatives of the African Union, and told them that some students at Swarthmore College wanted to raise money for their campaign to protect Darfuris from genocide. Would they take it? The African Union, like most armies, did not normally take money from private citizens, and it is hard to imagine that the leaders knew anything about Swarthmore. But they spent some time considering the matter, and decided they would make an exception and accept money from these students at Swarthmore College.

It is the rare student who is expected to fund an army of any sort, let alone one embarking on a peace mission, but Hanis was unfazed. He and his team received a memo of understanding with the African Union peacekeepers and started the campaign. They settled on $250,000 as a good target sum—large enough to seem significant, but not so large as to be impossible. Having never embarked on a formal fundraising campaign before, these college students consulted a few old hands, who explained that it was important to create a sense of urgency around any such campaign. Otherwise, people would put off making a donation until they finally forgot about it. So theirs was a "campaign for a hundred days"—a hundred days to take action in Darfur, Hanis said, and thus counter the previous hundred days of *in*action in Darfur, days that, in fact, closely resembled the hundred days of inaction before that, too. Again, the point wasn't just to raise money but to take political action, which Hanis knew from the beginning was the essential purpose.

That was phase one: defining the project. Then came the execution. And there Hanis and his colleagues got lucky—the kind of luck that comes from ample preparation. In the midst of the campaign, Hanis received a call from a woman whose name, Pam Omidyar, didn't quite register. She is the wife of eBay founder Pierre Omidyar, one of the world's wealthiest men, though Hanis didn't realize that at the time. "I didn't know who she was at all," Hanis says now, sheepishly. "She said, 'How can I help?'" Hanis told her what he was telling everybody, that what he really needed was money to buy pizza for his friends as they frantically emailed everyone they knew for money. Fine, the woman said, but surely there was more she could do than fund a pizza run. So Hanis rather tiredly said, Well, then, how about money for bus tickets from Swarthmore to DC? Nothing more "creative," Omidyar asked? So Hanis thought some more and asked her to come up with matching funds—$100 for every person he could get to travel to Washington so they could lobby. Not to protest, he emphasized. To lobby.

That was the whole idea. No humanitarian aid, no consciousness raising, no armbands. Instead, they wanted to deploy squadrons of politically savvy young believers to bombard legislators with demands to end the genocide in Darfur, or suffer the political consequences. "We'd tell our people, 'Put on your business suit and engage your policymakers in their offices about what they could do.'"

Impressed with the mission, Omidyar agreed. "And that's what we did," Hanis says. On the strength of her matching grant, Hanis got 440 tidied-up student lobbyists to descend on Washington to press the anti-genocide cause.

"I think she was impressed with this," Hanis says. Omidyar promptly sent a check for $44,000, and, of course, Hanis was impressed with that. That's when he thought maybe he should find out who she was. A Google search revealed the stunning truth. No fool, Hanis immediately got in touch with Omidyar to offer her a chance for greater involvement with his organization. He stressed the similarities between his organization and her foundation, Humanity United. After all, both appealed to the freshly empowered citizen, both were new, and both got results. Omidyar said she would wait and see. In 2005, after Hanis and his colleagues were able to raise the full $250,000 for the African Union in just a hundred days and simultaneously double the number of congressional cosponsors for a Darfur initiative, Omidyar got on board and became one of the Genocide Intervention Network's most important backers, donating a total of $1.2 million over its first three years.

As a new social entrepreneur, you might be wondering, So? What is the lesson? How can I ramp up and take my nonprofit to the next level? The answer is never obvious. No two nonprofits will ever do it the same way. There isn't a twelve-point checklist of things to get it done. As a rule, it is not a matter of doing more things so much as it is doing the same things differently, with greater scope and impact. In cultivating a donor like Pam Omidyar, Hanis was doing what any nonprofit would do: learning the needs and interests of its most important donors. As Hanis and his colleagues were scaling and developing their organization, it became more impressive to Omidyar and other seed donors. He did this knowing that a substantial gift from her would take the Genocide Intervention Network to the next level, allowing him to commit to it full-time and make it his life, which of course had a host of implications of its own.

It is, after all, one thing to run an organization like his as a kind of extracurricular activity while in college. It is another to take it on the road after graduation. But his progression follows the evolution of all nonprofits as they emerge from part-time, dining-table affairs to full-time, office-based businesses. The shift is not just a matter of style, but one of commitment. It's the difference between dating and marriage. The nonprofit becomes your life. That can be exhilarating, but it can be exhausting, too. Still full of idealism, Hanis decided on marriage.

"And so when we graduated," Hanis says, "we thought 'Wow! If we can do this much as students, imagine what we could do full-time!" Having identified donors, Hanis and a few colleagues could now ask them to help the Genocide Intervention Network "transition" from being a student group to a fully functioning nonprofit. Hanis and three other true believers rented an apartment together, which allowed them to socialize with each other during the rare breaks in their around-the-clock schedule. To survive, the four lived on what Hanis terms "survival stipends" that covered rent, food, and computers; their lives had precious little more. And they engaged in fundraising as if their professional lives depended on it, because they did.

The four of them graduated in May of 2005, and they gave themselves until December to make a go of it, or they'd bail and head to grad school or a paying job in the working world. Paradoxically, the fact that they had never done this before was their biggest asset. Ignorance is a kind of freedom, after all. And their youth brought them several advantages: they were not burdened by the families and mortgages of their older compatriots in the nonprofit movement, so they were more free to take risks; they needed fewer of the creature comforts that their elders were accustomed to; and at their age, they were naturally attuned to their fellow Gen Yers, who were the key ingredient of the "youth movement," as Hanis calls it, of people most receptive to the cause—and Hanis and his colleagues had a feeling for the social media that would reach them. They were convinced, too, that it was these unjaded young people who would supply the passion needed to shame senators and congressmen into making the fight against genocide a priority.

Before long, the very audaciousness of the enterprise started registering in places that could be helpful. There are foundations that specialize in supporting edgy, outside-the-box operations like Hanis's, much as venture capitalists would if his venture operated for profit. The more traction Hanis got among thought leaders, the more his anti-genocide operation was able to gain support from foundations like Ashoka, Echoing Green, and the Draper Richards Kaplan Foundation—some of it in the form of much-needed cash, and some in the form of even-more-needed technical support, providing expertise and the right candidates to fill out the nonprofit's board of directors. Remarkably, for an organization staffed by twenty-one-year-olds, the Genocide Intervention Network was able to attract a board of advisers that included Clinton's national security adviser Anthony Lake, the Africa specialist Gayle Smith, and the author who in some ways started it all, Samantha Power.

Attracting High-Profile Advisers

Seeing such a list, you might be wondering how you, too, can attract such luminaries to your start-up nonprofit. What was Hanis's secret? First, the heavyweights may not have known much about Hanis beyond his short resume, but they were very much drawn to his cause, and they were convinced that Hanis's organization had a chance of advancing it. Second, they couldn't help but be charmed by the Mouse That Roared quality of these young people who, while seemingly overmatched by the lions in Congress, were very businesslike and results oriented, the polar opposite of the pot-smoking tenderfoot. And they were impressed that Hanis and his compatriots were actually acting on their beliefs, not just spouting some rhetoric over lattes in Starbucks.

At every stage, though, Hanis and his team were thinking of what was next. From the earliest days, Hanis knew that this organization wasn't just about the horrors of Darfur. The more confined the cause, the more dismissible. Put another way, the bigger the aspiration, the more powerful and enduring it will be. But his ambitions had to be tempered by strategy. "We're not trying to stop every killing in every area in the world." Not because they don't want to, but because he realizes they can't. They have to be realistic, as strategy is always realistic. "We're taking off a bite at a time," he goes on. Now, five years later, Hanis has taken a lot more bites. "We're starting with Sudan. We've expanded to Congo and Burma. We're trying to expand to other areas. If someone were to point to me and say, 'He's working to stop genocide,' you might not want to engage. But I think if you actually had a conversation about how we do it, like with the (1-800-GENOCIDE) hotline, you'd be more inclined. We think about it very step-by-step, very strategically. You'd feel like, 'OK, they're not over their head. They're actually being strategic about rolling it out within their time constraints, their resources. And hopefully, with that, you'd get involved.'"

It is noteworthy that the Genocide Intervention Network got on the map when it attracted high-level advisers. Such advisers serve two functions. First, as illustrious people, they give a new organization luster just by associating with it. The rub-off effect. It can give a nonprofit instant gravitas, which can be essential. If you want to get on the map, get Condoleezza Rice on your board. Her name will do wonders, but her name may be all you can get. Some A-list advisers of this sort will actually give you some time advising, and that is of incalculable benefit, but don't count on it. Remember, though, that just because the person is illustrious doesn't mean he's good. Bernie Madoff was Jay Feinberg's chairman of the board for the Gift of Life for a brief time, but fortunately made none of the investment decisions. Other nonprofits now wish they had looked their gift horse a little closer in the mouth.

But such advisers, when they are working properly, can offer entrée to key areas of business or society, presenting essential ideas, giving the CEO invaluable private tutoring, offering the kind of wisdom that normally takes several decades to acquire. If he'd had it, Scott H. Silverman, for example, might have sought out a program like STRIVE, which provided the replicable curriculum that saved his organization, long before he stumbled across it on *60 Minutes*. And, as with the advisers from the Ashoka Foundation and others like it, these can come with dollars attached, as a welcome condition of a grant.

Your Organization Is Your Responsibility

Getting the right people to open their minds and their wallets to you can be invaluable. Every budding organization can benefit from the support of those with the right knowledge, contacts, and funds. That said, you need to realize that even the most credentialed advisers aren't infallible. The most elite minds in economics haven't been able to maintain the nation's financial prosperity. So keep your wits about you. Keep asking questions. Take nothing at face value. Check the advice of one against that of another, listen for incongruities, and don't be afraid to ask questions. Although you do need the support of others, in the end, for good or ill, it is your organization, and you will be accountable for its results.

CHAPTER 8

Setting Goals and Keeping on Track

Start Small and Grow

AN ORGANIZATION'S MISSION IS ITS ASPIRATION—it says what you are trying to achieve. It stems from the concept that first brought you into the field, that flash of inspiration that got your heart going. But aspiration and inspiration aren't enough. You need to set goals. Goals are the immediate targets for your aspiration. They should be practical, believable, and communicable. By now, you've moved on from the dream and started to engage with the reality. The goal now is not what you dream of doing, but what you actually can do.

Hanis and company were masterful at setting goals, starting with a small achievable one and then enlarging their ambitions as their capabilities increased. For all Hanis's protests that he wasn't directly targeting the elimination of genocide, just the name of Genocide Intervention Network suggests otherwise. In expanding his scope, he is departing from most organizations, which too often overshoot and have to rein themselves in. When a cancer group, say, realizes that it can't cure all cancer, it then specializes in curing one particular tumor. And when that cure is too large a goal, it focuses on its treatment, or one aspect of its treatment, and so on.

Although Hanis's may be unusual among all nonprofits, his trajectory is standard for the successful ones that populate this book. Start small and keep growing. Of course, there are constraints as to just how much growth you can achieve. Even the Bill & Melinda Gates Foundation, with its almost unlimited budget, has focused its efforts on a relatively few project areas, where clear, demonstrable progress is possible. Certain goals are simply beyond the scope of even the most ambitious nonprofit. But, as in any field, if you do well, you'll do more; if you do not do so well, you'll do less and maybe a lot less. With success, you gain attention, win greater resources, and can expand your reach. Along the way, you are likely to increase your capabilities, too, and you may be eager for the economies of scale that come with expansion. No longer will you think locally; instead you will increasingly think globally. Hanis's eyes may have grown wide, but so have Rebecca Onie's as she has expanded Health Leads to five other cities, Michael Brown's as he takes his City Year all across the country, Robert Carmona's as he goes national with STRIVE, and Anne Heyman's as she looks to take her youth village to other countries with heavy orphan populations.

Milo Cutter: Bringing Goals into Focus

Goals, though necessary, can be slow to announce themselves. Minnesota schoolteacher Milo Cutter, for example, did not wake up one morning thinking that she would start the first charter school in the nation. No, she just believed that a number of the students in her classes at her St. Paul high school where she had taught for four years (she'd spent almost twenty years in the land title business before that) needed a different type of high school from the standard, crowded, loud one. As she says, "It wasn't 'Oh,

110

let's start a school that would be the first charter.' There was a need, and that's what we followed."

Only gradually did her path become clear. Her sister mentioned that she'd seen that Minnesota had recently created a new category of school in the state, something called a charter school, that would be free of many of the constraints of standard public schools. Intrigued, Cutter called the state commissioner for education, who said that her sister had it right: the legislature had indeed passed such legislation, but no one had yet come forth to take the state up on it. He said she should check with the district superintendent in St. Paul. He tried to discourage her, as anything *new* wasn't all that appealing to him. The idea of starting a new school that kept the kids' interests uppermost in mind continued to bang around in Cutter's head, though. She tried more conventional schemes, realized they were probably nonstarters, but kept thinking about the misfits in her school, a term that, absent the pejorative, applied to so many of the students she knew. A standard-issue public high school seemed too big for them and too impersonal. "There were too many people for them to talk to any of them," Cutter says. "The kids were intimidated, and felt unsuccessful." The curriculum didn't seem made for them, either. She kept returning to this idea of a charter.

Cutter's goal was to devise a school that met the students' needs. That meant the kids came first, and to an astonishing extent, they decided what the school would be like. Did the administration and faculty design the school? "Oh no, we didn't design it," Cutter quickly replies, appalled at the idea. "The students designed it. They made it. Everything that's there in our school came from what they've said to us—and still do."

She gives a small, telling example. Early on, she felt obligated to bring a lawyer in to draw up the school's bylaws. In the course of the discussion, the lawyer asked about the student handbook, which lays out the rules for student behavior. Cutter almost didn't understand the question. What rules, she wanted to know. "Well, you have to have the rules about they can't do this and can't do that," she recalls the lawyer saying. "And I told her, 'Well, that's not where we are going with this.'"

She bid the lawyer adieu, turned to the students, and told them what the woman had said, explaining that Cutter personally wasn't fond of "Don'ts," as she put it. So she asked them, "What do you want? What do you want the school to look like?" In the end, the handbook just boiled down to one word, Cutter says. *Respect*. "The students wanted respect."

And so it went. The school would be small, just fifty-three kids, the better to give each one personal attention. The students and staff would call each other by their first names "because the school is the transition point to adult roles," Cutter says. Students and staff would all sit together for lunch. No staff lounge. "It's the students first," she says. Not the teachers. The school would not be housed in any conventional school building, but in a recreation center. It was available during the day and would be kid-friendly and have a great vibe. "Our students like them," she explains of recreation centers. "They're safe places. They're welcoming. We aren't going to have metal detectors greeting people, or security guards." She pauses. "There aren't many things around here where we didn't sit and bang our heads against the wall and say, 'Why?'" So by adhering to the working principle of "students first," Cutter found her mission. Sharp as Cutter's initial vision may have seemed to her, sharp as all initial visions may seem, it wasn't really clear until she built it—and they started to come. Such visions are the opposite of mirages: they become more real the closer you come to them. They teach you what you need to do.

Keep Your Goals Aligned with Your Mission

What should be your goal? Ideally, of course, the goal you end up with should align with the vision that brought you into nonprofits in the first place. That was the case with Cutter, and she's still pumped up about it, almost twenty years later. It only makes sense to stick with what excited and motivated you to undertake this most Herculean of tasks. You're going to need that enthusiasm. But sometimes the facts on the ground require some adjustments. Cutter was able to keep whittling away at her dream until she found the reality within it, but that's unusual. Oftentimes, reality is not what you expect it to be. The funding may be insufficient to fulfill your ambition, or there can be a shortfall in the capabilities of your organization or, more alarmingly, in your own capabilities. The staff, directors, or funders you enlist may see the project differently than you do—and they might be right. This can inspire a serious rethinking. You shouldn't necessarily jump to plan B; the organization needs to keep its original animating vision. But you may consider plan A1.

Like athletes, social entrepreneurs can play offense or defense, and offense is better. An aggressive, action-oriented approach is the only way to advance a cause. How to stay on offense? One way is by infusing the organization with an inspirational sense of purpose. Remember that as the leader, you must be so fully identified with the mission that to deny it would be to deny yourself, and vice versa. This is true of all eighteen of our social entrepreneurs, and it explains a great deal of their success. Mark Hanis, Milo Cutter, Scott H. Silverman—their drive stems from their unique backgrounds, yet their drive also catches up the aspirations of countless others. They serve as both proxies and mirrors, representing themselves and their constituents. This can create tremendous social energy to get things done.

If you do correct your course, say so. Don't try to pretend you haven't. Nonprofits depend on the harmony that comes from full and open communication, so get the word out. If the identity of the institution seems to be up for grabs, with some people thinking it is all about this, others saying it is all about that, you're inviting chaos. Don't. Your organization can be about only one thing.

Geoffrey Canada: Measuring and Reassessing Goals

Handsome, well-spoken, magnetic Geoffrey Canada, the president and CEO of the Harlem Children's Zone, has now achieved celebrity status through extensive media coverage, including an American Express ad campaign and an appearance in the powerful documentary film *Waiting for "Superman."* But his school faced an institutional identity crisis back in 1996, and it nearly broke the organization apart. At that point, like most social entrepreneurs, he had just about everything invested in it. It is not too much to say that he'd begun the work back when he was eleven and attended PS 99 in the South Bronx, one of the most disadvantaged areas of New York City. That year, he started to notice that his schoolmates fell into two distinct groups—the ones who were going someplace, and the ones who weren't. How'd he know? He figured out the school's tracking system. The kids who'd gotten onto the fast track in his second-grade class, section 2-1, stayed in the top section all the way through. The kids at the bottom of second grade, in 2-8, never climbed out of it. "There was no way to go from 2-8 into 3-1," he says, referring to the kids' move to third grade. The best they could do was go from 2-8 to 3-7, just one rung up. "But even that was difficult."

That was, as he says, "the school part." There was also "the nonschool part," and that was the way these slow-track kids lived. "I could see that our community was falling apart, and it was destroying kids every day. The drugs, the violence, the lack of adult intervention, the lack of opportunities for kids to do anything except stay on the street corners." The nonschool part fed the school part, and vice versa. "I could see both processes whittling down the number of children who were ever going to make it out of there in any kind of healthy or productive way."

Canada and his brothers were a case in point. Their father had disappeared when the boys were very young, leaving their mother on welfare. She was still determined to do the best by her sons, and managed to get Canada's oldest brother Dan out of 5-8 to a better class, and it made all the difference. He is now an engineer in a nuclear facility. Likewise, Geoffrey Canada was on the fast track, and stayed on it through high school, all the way to a full scholarship at Bowdoin and graduate school at the Harvard School of Education.

Canada went into education; after a stint as a high school principal, he worked for two years in a mental health program, and then came to the Harlem Children's Zone in 1983. At the time, it was called the Rheedlen Centers for Children and Families. It had a different formula, but its intentions were the same as now: to give the children of Harlem the same chances in life that other American children had. Canada believed that he had the tools. He'd taught at a quasi-charter school, and he figured that the mental health job gave him insights into the psychological underpinnings of a community. As he rose up through the ranks at Rheedlen, he hoped to put this knowledge to use in breaking the cycle of poverty in Harlem. Eventually, he was hired to run the place.

At Rheedlen, everything looked fine. It was clicking along on plan A. "We thought we were doing a good job," Canada says.

"Everybody was telling us we were doing a good job." But the academic in him wanted proof, so he commissioned an elaborate series of tests to see if Rheedlen was indeed as good as everyone said. Unfortunately, the test results said no, it was not. Not nearly. When the actual outcomes of Rheedlen's graduates were compared to a control group of similar kids outside the school, they showed that Rheedlen had almost no effect at all. "By any of the indicators we cared about—graduation rates, college admissions rates, incarceration rates—our kids were doing as bad as, if not worse than, they were when I began in 1983." Some of it was non-school related: the epidemic of crack cocaine and escalating violence. But that wasn't much consolation. "We worked really, really hard, and we failed," Canada says.

The bottom line was that the kids weren't any better off for attending Rheedlen, and that fact needed to be faced. Clearly, the goals needed to be reassessed. The mission wouldn't change—Rheedlen would keep working to give inner-city kids a better shot at decent lives—but the immediate goals would be different, shifting away from a focus on just getting students to graduate high school to getting them into and through college and then placed in good jobs after graduation.

Canada recounts his thought process. "It was at that point that we had to consider the next thing, which was, 'Do I believe it's impossible to do what we are trying to do?'" He wasn't having any of that. "Obviously, the answer was no. We thought we could be successful, the kids could be successful. So what do I have to do differently to make that happen?" He turns contemplative.

It is at the point of the rationalization of the data and the acceptance of it that I think that most people struggle and fail. If you spend all of your time trying to prove that it's not really as bad as it is, and people do—or, deciding that

116

it really is bad then simply walking away from the problem, shrugging and saying, "Well, look, we tried, but there's nothing you can do about this," which a lot of people do. They just accept failure. We'll help the kids we can, and most of the others aren't going to make it.

So the real challenge for people who care about these issues is—how do you confront something that's not working and say, "We have to come up with a more powerful strategy?" And it took about a week of agonizing—and I know that some people will think that was short, and others think it long—but that is about what it took. At first people wrung their hands and said that can't be true. We're working much too hard. It's got to be better than that. But probably about the fourth or fifth day, a group of us got together and said, "OK, you know what, guys? This ain't working. And we're going to have to come up with a better strategy."

Now, I will say there is some cost in doing that. Meaning, if people have supported a cause, you worry about whether they will now walk away. What will people say? Are they going to stick with us if we tell the truth about this? How rapidly do we let people know? But all of that I think is procedural. And the real challenge is, Are you prepared to look at the data and then accept that we actually can do something?

So, what did they decide to do? To go not to plan B but to plan A. To change just about everything, including the name, but leave the core mission untouched. The Rheedlen Centers had been intended to save Harlem kids by providing a transformative educational experience. In Canada's estimation, that didn't go far enough. Rheedlen operated as though high school were a booster

117

shot—an injection of a terrific four years. But he could see that it took more than a brilliant high school experience. It wasn't going to begin with freshman year and end at graduation. It required an inspiring after-school experience. The students didn't need a terrific school as much as they needed a different environment, one that was safe, nurturing, and stimulating. And they needed this at home, on the street, at their friends' houses. Only by reaching out into the community would he hope to make the difference he sought. The point was never just to get kids through high school. It was, as he says, "to end generational poverty—and that will never happen with just a high school diploma."

To mark the transformation, the Rheedlen Centers would eventually be renamed the Harlem Children's Zone (HCZ)—"Zone" because it was providing a zone of nurturance for Harlem children that would be surprisingly all-encompassing. If Rheedlen had been bent on creating a shelter that would get kids through a storm, the HCZ was a kind of expansive greenhouse that protected them from the elements even as it let the sunshine through.

Once it became clear that the Rheedlen Centers were meeting the wrong goal, Canada set about identifying the right one. And that meant a new business plan, which was created with the assistance of Bridgespan, an organization dedicated to giving nonprofits like Canada's the tools to succeed. Bridgespan guided the organization to redesign its operation, expanding the scope of its activities radically. As the consultants pointed out, halfway measures would not get them even halfway. If the mission was to end generational poverty, then the program would have to continue through college. Only college graduates could truly lift themselves, their children, and possibly even their neighbors out of poverty.

To mold the kind of kids who would succeed in college, Canada determined that he would have to start very early, literally in the womb through an early-development parenting program dubbed the Baby College®. That is followed by an all-day pre-K program that prepares children for kindergarten. In its Peacemakers program, HCZ trains young people to work as teaching assistants and role models in local public schools and after-school programs. Because of the high rates of asthma in the inner city, HCZ created an Asthma Initiative to help asthmatic children reduce the number of school absences, emergency room visits, and hospitalizations that too often attend the disease. And on it goes for HCZ: free health and nutrition classes and physical activities for middle schoolers; job-related technology classes for teens and young adults; college guidance to help college students stay focused and on track; crisis intervention services like anger management and communication workshops for families in distress.

New goals require new methods, and Canada had to ramp up his fundraising efforts substantially. Here Canada's inherent charisma has paid off. Blessed with uncommon communication skills, Canada has been able to draw sufficient contributions to turn a $3.5 million operation when he took over in 1990[1] to nearly a $75 million operation in 2010.[2] As of 2011, the HCZ had an astonishing $132 million endowment,[3] one that Canada is hoping to push past $300 million. To him, that is what it takes to make a long-term investment in future students, who are being born every day. And what is his pitch? He goes on the offense. "I say to people that we are really designing a program that is going to win. And that is after years spent trying to figure out how little we could lose. No one's been really trying to win. No one's gone in and said, 'Let's figure out a way to end the cycle of poverty.'"

And the dream just gets bigger. He is relying on his students to inspire others in Harlem, and counting on the uplift of his HCZ to encourage other organizations in Harlem to do their part. He's helped create tenant associations and block associations to clean up local parks and playgrounds, and he's even taken on issues that may seem tangential but aren't to him—such as obesity, encouraging programs of exercise and proper nutrition, and dental health, pushing for regular checkups.

Ultimately, Canada is creating a place apart, one that intends to raise up not just the children but everyone in it. It is such a huge goal that it runs the risk of being not just unreachable but incomprehensible. It is hard to know if "goal" is even the right word. "People keep trying to make us fish or fowl," Canada admits. "Some people consider us a school; others look at our comprehensive services. I'm not sure if what we are doing is new, but it is different. Mostly, people define it by what they are advocating for themselves. If they are for wraparound services, they see ours as that. If they are for schools, they see this as a school initiative. Interestingly enough, the person who seemed to get this the best was President Obama, who saw it as everything."

In having the HCZ be everything, of course, Canada runs the risk of its being nothing, which is the nonprofit equivalent of mission creep, and it can overextend a nonprofit just as it does an army. In Canada's case, his own success is possibly his greatest hazard. He is such an attractive personality and such a prodigious fundraiser that he is not constrained by the same financial limits that others are. This, combined with his ever widening definition of success, has allowed him to keep growing his operation. The best-known cure for mission creep, ironically, is the strict measurement that got him started down the road to the HCZ in the first place.

Getting on Track and Staying There

When they've lost track of their location, lost sight of their destination, and don't know whether to go to the left or to the right, many nonprofits have turned to outside firms to serve as a kind of GPS for lost social entrepreneurs. And one of the things they are likely to do to get on course, as was true with Canada, is to revise their business plan. Such a plan need not be long. About five pages is the norm. It is the essence of the nonprofit and, as such, needs to be short, crisp, and very much to the point. It normally consists of a concise summary of the mission, ideally in a short, electrifying paragraph that states the social need and the unique solution offered by the proposed new entity. For Rebecca Onie's Project HEALTH, the statement, as formulated for her business plan, was a single, jam-packed sentence:

Project HEALTH works to break the link between poverty and poor health by mobilizing college students to provide sustained public health interventions in partnership with urban medical centers, universities, and community organizations.[4]

The mission statement is followed by the business plan itself—how the organization will be funded and by whom; the likely client base; and expenses, both in terms of overhead and marginal costs, expressed per individual served. It should contain all the essential financial details that anyone would want to see to be assured that the venture is sound and sensible. Costs and expenses need not be in balance initially—that's where philanthropy comes in. But funders like to see a route to the break-even point.

All of that should fit on the first page because, let's face it, few people have the patience to go further, especially if the plan has been presented for them to flip through during a meeting, as is often the case. If they were to soldier on for the remaining pages, they would find an elaboration of the essential elements, perhaps a classification of the different donor groups expected to participate, or a look at the demographics and geographical distribution of the potential clientele. And after that would come the charts, graphs, and other visual information that would buttress the argument and, ideally, demonstrate a certain Wow factor that will impress potential investors.

Crafting a good business plan is not an idle exercise: it is the seed from which the organization grows. And if that organization goes awry, as it did for Canada, such a plan can bring it back into alignment with its aspirations. Likewise, a business plan can serve to elucidate a nonprofit's adjusted or expanded mission, as it did for Rebecca Onie's Project HEALTH, now known as Health Leads. Onie relied on what she termed a strategic plan to lift her organization's sights after it had outgrown its initial operational niche. She sought to transition her organization from one that was working solely to expand the definition of medicine for the poor in six cities to one that was also making an impact on national health policy. "Everybody makes such a big deal of starting organizations, but I think the hardest work is sustaining and developing and deepening the impact of high-quality organizations. The launch is a unique insight and a pairing of need with a solution. But beyond that, the stakes aren't as high as they are later."

The expansion into new cities brought new vigor and new fundraising opportunities to the operation, but Onie reached further and sought to become what she terms a "compelling proof point" that Medicare and Medicaid might look to in deciding which medical services would be reimbursable to the poor, thus making Health Leads a possible model for an expanded definition of care all across the country. More than merely ambitious, this expanded scope pulls Health Leads from the realm of the physical to something approaching the metaphysical. It switches from caregivers performing a service to a demonstration project promoting the *idea* of that service. That, of course, would shift Health Leads's objectives dramatically in a new direction—toward providing evidence through benchmarking, data collection, evaluation, and metric refinement, and then promoting the findings nationally through public relations lobbying. And, of course, toward massive fundraising to support it all. Hence the strategic plan, which was designed to lay out the rationale—chiefly increased impact—for raising $11.1 million to fund the transition.

But, again, even though Onie's goals have shifted, her fundamental mission—to broaden the definition of medicine to include such essentials as good nutrition, decent shelter, and the like—has not. It is this very stability that has allowed the organization to move forward into uncharted waters with such confidence and dispatch.

Staying on Course

For any start-up, whether for-profit or nonprofit, the seas are big and the boat pretty small. The key thing is to know where you are and where you are trying to go. Although the plan may grow and the goals may shift, the mission can serve to keep the organization on course. It is like the keel on a sailboat. Without it, the boat will drift helplessly, at the mercy of every breeze; with it, the boat can cut through the water with confidence, even in the stiffest gale.

CHAPTER 9

Staffing Up

Your Most Vexing Resource: People!

JUST AS YOUR FIRST CHILD makes you a parent, your first employee will make you a manager, even while you are still growing the operation. And just as children often need at least some parenting well into their adult lives, employees have been known to require supervision regardless of their seniority. Of all your activities running your organization, handling people is bound to be the most vexing. Puzzling as a spreadsheet can be, a human being is infinitely more complex—by turns flighty, inspired, petulant, generous, dopey, brilliant, oversensitive, insightful, and uppity. The standard nonprofit is a people-to-people business. That is one of its joys; it can also be one of its frustrations.

What makes managing employees so hard? Everything! It is easier to say what doesn't. Unlike for-profits, nonprofits lack the financial inducement of serious money—salaries, bonuses, raises—to attract the most desirable employees and to reward the best performance. A senior staffer who commands $500,000 in the private sector would be doing well to make $150,000 at a nonprofit, and $100,000 would not be unreasonable. That deprives managers of an important motivational tool—and can present a problem if staff members are constantly feeling financially stressed. But nonprofits can also create an environment that is nearly unique in the landscape

125

of American business, one where people are drawn to the enterprise not for the money they'll make but for the meaning they'll find.

Darell Hammond: Creating a Good Place to Work

Nonprofits would be wise to play up the fact that employees have entered a place like no other, one that is almost magical for being so different. Here at the Andrea and Charles Bronfman Philanthropies, we have filled the halls and offices with cheerful and festive sculpture and paintings. People often say that it is like an art gallery; they also say that they have never seen anything like it. The point is to delight and to inspire, and we think it does. At Darell Hammond's KaBOOM!, the colors let you know you're in for something different the moment you step inside the front door. The office is painted a startling purple and orange. "Even if you came here at night or on a weekend when no one was around," says Hammond, "you could pick up on the culture of this place, that it's all about fun and play." The spirited environment, along with a collaborative ethic, has been a key to KaBOOM!'s success; it is as distinctive as the exclamation mark at the end of its name. But it's not just the paint. KaBOOM! brings some of the cheer of the playground to the enterprise, as it is relatively unstructured, depends on cooperation (facilitated by the shared-space cubicles), and fosters creativity. "Joy, wonder, collaboration, we're all in it together," says Hammond. "These are the qualities we're going for at KaBOOM!" And it seems to be working. KaBOOM! has won high praise as a workplace from the *NonProfit Times,* and employees sometimes call it a "utopia." And it's not just KaBOOM! Most nonprofits are, hour for hour, far more enjoyable places to work than for-profits, as they offer more flexible hours, greater autonomy, fuller engagement, and a more humane environment.

Hammond realizes that the culture at KaBOOM! isn't for everyone, however. "We have to lay out our expectations up front, so we aren't springing anything on anybody. And we have to get the right people, the ones who are oriented to our way of doing things." This is true for all organizations. You need to create an environment that will attract the people who are right for you, and the nature of that environment will vary from place to place. But if you get it right and get the right people, then, as Hammond notes, "it becomes an all-in proposition, not just a management proposition." They buy it, in short. And that's good news.

Where to Start

In gathering the key individuals who are going to advance your cause, be careful and go slowly, for it is much easier to hire than to fire. Obviously, you can't know everything about a person before you bring him on board, so focus on those areas of his personality and background that you consider essential. It goes without saying that the person should possess all the qualities needed for any job: sterling work history, relevant experience, impressive reputation, and so on. But, also true for any job, the personal qualities are probably more important—and harder to get at.

Begin with generalists, people who can do everything and are happy to. They'll answer the phone, clean the bathroom, and deftly soothe a major donor over the phone. As you grow, your hires will become more specialized, addressing particular needs. But whether they are social workers, accountants, or receptionists, they will need to maintain a special rapport with you and with the purposes of the organization. Scott H. Silverman, of Second Chance, says that his background in retail shaped his hiring attitudes by teaching him the value of customer service. Without good service, a business can lose customers and ultimately be imperiled. "So getting good people has always been an issue. I want to find people who *want* to be good. Those, to me, are good people."

Until fairly recently, all of Silverman's employees were themselves graduates of his Second Chance program. "We had this policy that if you weren't an ex-felon, you couldn't work with me," he says. "They have a tried-and-true experience in life that you can't get in a four-year university, and you can't get in a weekend seminar of walking on hot coals."

It's one thing to hire well-meaning employees, and it is another to get them to follow through on the ambitions of the organization. And here Silverman prides himself in his ability to get all of his employees on the same page with that. "One of the nicest compliments I think we get most consistently about our agency is not about how much money we raise or how many people we serve. No, the thing I hear most is how in God's name do you get everyone to say the same thing all the time? How do we all end up speaking the same language?" The answer is that he doesn't force a line on anyone. He just hires people who get it automatically. The message doesn't enter the brain at the ear, but at a point lower down in the limbic system. "We call it the twelve-inch trip from your heart to your head. Everything we do here is heart driven. The words people use to describe it are their own; it's not a recitation of a sound bite. It's more like a gut feeling, from down deep. It's an automatic response. It's the way we treat people, and I guess it's how we want to be treated ourselves. And it's key to everything we do, because we're dealing with so many different people with so many different barriers that the whole thing would fall apart otherwise."

Implicit in this description is a critical aspect of hiring, namely the need to find people who are eager to learn and to grow with the organization. Everyone makes mistakes; the question is, can she learn from them? Silverman himself likes to say that he expects mistakes, but would prefer that they be made quickly so that everyone can learn from them right away. The prospect of excellence should serve as motivation, first to encourage a keening for it and second so that it is appreciated when it is present. You want people to enjoy a job well done; such satisfaction will keep them going.

Things to Consider

Another principle in hiring is the Socratic injunction, know thyself. Or, more exactly, know thy weaknesses and deficiencies, and hire to cover them. When you're starting out, you need to be sure to add staff members whose skills complement, rather than duplicate, yours. We're not convinced that the brain divides neatly between a creative side and an analytical side, but we do believe that whichever you have less of, you need more of, so bolster your deficiencies through your hires. No individual will exhibit a perfect balance of the creative and the analytical, but the organization as a whole should. One staffer can be the big ideas person, but don't forget to have someone who can do payroll. So if you know that you are good at grand conceptual thinking but are terrible at details like taking care of your email account, by all means hire a detail person to cover for you. That way, all the emails get read, the critical info is gleaned from them, and they are promptly responded to. Likewise, if you are a little shy around people—a serious liability in most nonprofits—hire someone more outgoing who will love people up for you.

As your organization grows, you will start to recruit professional staff—people with a master's in social work or an MBA from a business school that offers programs for work in nonprofits. One of the most important requirements is that they all buy in to the mission. You might imagine that the paid staff members at the lower end of the scale aren't likely to be involved in the mission, but they usually are. The professionals will evaluate the mission, too. It will be a key factor in their decision. If they are in, they are in, and will likely become eager and effective spokespeople for the organization wherever they go. One caveat: if yours is a risk-taking organization, make sure your staff are risk-takers themselves. Otherwise, expect trouble down the road.

In the hiring process, a potential employee also needs to be told exactly what is expected of her and how she fits into the larger picture of the organization. She should have the purpose of the organization down cold, not just knowing it but believing in it. And, once hired, the employee should be comfortable doing her job—and with asking questions if she isn't. Finally, standards need to be laid out so that employees are clear as to how they are to be evaluated, whether it is on a quarterly, semiannual, or yearly basis.

The staff need to be complementary to you in terms of skills, but they're going to need to be like you when it comes to time commitment. If you're going full out to get the nonprofit running or to keep it running, and you're accustomed to spending eighty-hour weeks and thinking nothing of it, you would be advised not to hire staff who think forty hours a week is plenty. Conversely, if you would like to get home to your family by six, you'd be wise not to hire a Mr. Compulsive who likely won't turn off the office lights until nine.

You can't take enough care. We recommend psychological testing of the candidates who have reached the final round of any job search. Here at the Andrea and Charles Bronfman Philanthropies, we generally prefer that every candidate take a psychological test, such as the Myers-Briggs, to give us a basic understanding of where she is coming from. We find the Myers-Briggs most helpful because of its focus on the continuum of extroversion to introversion, a key dynamic for group cohesion. We can't have too many showboats or too many mice. Compared to for-profit operations, nonprofits tend to be considerably more public; almost like government agencies, they work person-to-person. We find that the personality type that is likely to be most successful in the nonprofit realm is somewhere near the midpoint between intro- and extroversion. Too much extroversion, and the candidate has too little self-awareness; too much introversion, and he is closed to others.

But we add questions of our own. One is, "Tell me the thing in the last year you're most proud of." We word it just like that, deliberately leaving it open as to whether this is something the candidate has done, witnessed, or merely heard about, whether it is in business or in her personal life. The answer can be very revealing, as it tells a lot about where she places her focus and how she defines what makes her proud. Because they are so open ended, hypothetical questions help us get a glimpse into the candidate's thinking processes, another important variable. And we always like to meet the candidate's spouse or significant other. Whether the candidate is deferential, haughty, superficial, or joking—the way she interacts with her other half can tell us a lot about her approach to relationships. We're not particularly interested in the candidate's inner life, which we will probably never get to know anyway. We just want to know if we can work with her. But keep in mind that although Myers-Briggs and other similar tests can be useful, a test is still only one tool; it's imprecise. We would never depend on it to choose one candidate over another, but we think it is a great way to gain confidence in a choice we've already made.

One thing about hiring we cannot emphasize enough: whoever you hire will never look better to you than she does during her final job interview. For it is then that she has most on the line and is putting everything she has into every moment, to persuade you that she is indeed the best person for the job. So never hire anyone on the assumption that he will "grow into the job." Baloney. Nobody ever does. It goes only downward from there. Jeff will never forget the woman who was in the running for a CEO position for a program in New York. Jeff was serving as an outside nonboard adviser. The search was down to the final two; and, for the final interview, he noticed that the female candidate, ostensibly the more qualified one, showed up with wet hair. All he could think was, *Is that the best she can do for the most important job interview of her life to date?* He voted against her, but the three others on the selection committee voted for her. And she was a disaster, utterly disorganized, unfocused, late—everything that the wet hair predicted. She was gone in just over a year.

You also should recognize that making choices becomes progressively more difficult the larger the organization grows. The first hire means that the company is just you, A, and another person, B. Your relationship is bilateral. Hire again, and the relationships don't just double, they triple. For you will have to deal with both B and C, and with this new B–C dyad, which offers the added complication of outnumbering you. Add D to the mix, and you have your three private relationships with B, C, and D, and they each have relationships with each other, which have their own set of ever shifting dynamics. By the time you get to a half-dozen employees, still a small organization by most standards, you have created a spider's web of interrelationships, each of them prone to change by the day if not by the hour or minute.

Darell Hammond: Managing Relationships

It is hard to divine the subtle interplays of the many ingredients in such a rich stew. Still, this unique aggregate of personalities makes up the culture of your organization. Once established, that culture is altered only slowly, if at all. Yet it is probably the single biggest determinant of an organization's success. Hammond calls his a culture of sharing, and it stems from the all-in, participatory ethic that is represented by the bright colors and the array of cubicles in a shared space. "From the very beginning, we were disseminating knowledge and research papers in our manuals in hard copy for people who requested them," he says. "Now, of course, with the Internet, there's been a deluge of information about *other* ways of building a playground, not just ours, and we want our people to think about the other ways so that we maybe can come up with a better way." He goes on: "There's an idea culture here that the best ideas can come from anybody at any time. And they won't necessarily come from me. In fact, if they do come only from me, we haven't got the right people on the bus to get the job done."

And when a business relationship goes awry? It is not easy to get it back on track again. Back in the early days, Hammond was completely at sea when it came time to address an employee issue. Like many young founders, he had only his summer jobs to fall back on. "I had no real management experience before I was the CEO and founder of an organization. So the way I used to manage people was to sit them down in a conference room and say, 'You didn't do this right. You didn't do that right.'" He assumed that such comments would be enough to make sure that the particular mistake was never repeated, by that employee or by anyone else. This assumption was, of course, erroneous; worse, his approach hurt morale and sapped the energy that the organization could bring to the tasks ahead. "Now, when I look back, I cringe, because it wasn't them who needed to change. It was me." Now, when Hammond seeks to improve an employee's performance, he focuses far less on what the person has done wrong and far more on what he or she might do right; this is a conversation they have together, working toward a common solution that will encourage them both. "It's all about providing feedback that is constructive and meaningful and actionable," he says.

More broadly, a founder should strive to create the sort of environment where such feedback is less and less necessary. The work environment and culture should be enough to provide the cues necessary for the employees to succeed—without too much intervention by the founder. It's a system that is almost Darwinian, in that it relies on the idea that each participant will find his or her niche and operate seamlessly there. Far easier said than done, this can only be a goal, not an expectation. But it does offer a vision of how employees can vex a little less and contribute a little more.

It's All About Choosing the Right People

Silverman and Hammond, so different in their hiring practices in most respects, were alike in this one: each of them chose employees who were right for them. No employee is going to be right for every job, and it takes a lot of thought to define exactly what sort of person you seek for a post and to recognize that a particular candidate is perfect—or really isn't. Anyone who has ever hired someone will tell you that it is a humbling experience, and the constraints of the nonprofit world make it no easier. Arduous as it can be to select an employee, that's just the beginning. Then there's the work. Like any company, a nonprofit is only as good as its employees. Their energy, along with yours, will make it what it is.

CHAPTER 10

Hard Knocks

Weathering the Storms

ONE OF THE BEAUTIFUL THINGS ABOUT working in nonprofits is that they attract people who are passionate about the cause rather than those who are motivated solely by money. But trying to manage an organization that runs largely on passion can be more than a little tricky, for that passion is not always put in service to full agreement with the direction of the leadership. When passionate people disagree, they do so loudly, with lots of bombast and vitriol that can be damaging to a young organization.

All young organizations take their hard knocks. Your organization becomes bigger than you. Things don't always go according to plan, and people don't always agree, and you certainly don't always see the trouble coming. But if you stay calm and remain focused on your goal, you should be able to weather the storms.

Darell Hammond: The Coup

Darell Hammond calls it "the coup." More exactly, it was an *attempted* coup, but the incident was rattling nonetheless. It came about because of his faith in a key employee. Misplaced faith. It was one of those moments that, as a young social entrepreneur, you are all too likely to face at some point. Your nonprofit is up and running; you're starting to relax and congratulate yourself. Everything is fine—until, suddenly, it isn't. Your dreams are clobbered by reality. You have to come to terms with your ambitions quickly, or they may be gone.

Overly dramatic? Maybe. But not for Hammond. To him, his coup felt like something out of a banana republic, when the president returns from vacation to discover a general sitting in his executive chair, automatic in hand. Indeed, it occurred in part because a nonprofit *is* a little like a banana republic, albeit a benign one, with a strong leader and, too often, a shaky infrastructure, messy backroom politics, loose regulation, uncertain services, and scarce resources.

In Hammond's case, you had to add in the fact that he himself was just twenty-six, and unused to the sort of mendacity that his elders expect to crop up when large egos pursue scant power. KaBOOM! was growing efficiently, but Hammond decided that he would be the one flying about the country wooing corporate chieftains for funds to keep the growth going. In his absence, he entrusted the day-to-day management to a thirty-something managing director—call him Nicolo Machiavelli—who sported degrees from a pair of prestigious business and public policy schools. Before being hired, Machiavelli had done some contract work for KaBOOM! Everyone thought of him as a proven commodity.

When something is off in an organization, you often sense it before there is any obvious evidence. Previously, when Hammond returned from his ventures into corporation-land, he was greeted warmly, practically with back slaps and a pint of stout. That time, the reception seemed far less effusive, almost chilly. "The feeling just wasn't the same." Was he imagining things? No. It turned out that Machiavelli was figuratively measuring the drapes in Hammond's office. He delivered a letter to the chairman of the board saying that either Hammond had to go or Machiavelli would go, taking eight of the twelve staffers with him. He named the eight, further scorching the earth by placing practically the entire organization on the line.

The next board meeting had "100 percent attendance," Hammond jokes. They let Machiavelli speak his piece: Hammond was gone too often, too green, and so on. Then they gave the founder his turn to rebut the charges. He generously conceded the legitimacy of some claims—he copped to being young—and fiercely rejected others. When both sides were talked out, the board deliberated, and decided that although Machiavelli raised some valuable points, it was certainly not going to sanction an insurrection on the strength of them.

"The board wasn't going to be held hostage," sums up Hammond. The board gave Hammond its blessing if he wanted to terminate Machiavelli's contract, which he promptly did. While he was at it, he told the eight would-be renegade staffers that although he would miss them if they left, they were free to go, too. Interestingly, only two took him up on that—and not for several months. There, the crisis ended.

In such a crisis, there is the sensible way to respond, and the not-sensible way. To his credit, Hammond chose the former, although the latter was sorely tempting. The not-sensible way would be to be outraged not only at Machiavelli but also at the eight errant employees for their disloyalty. The sensible way was for him to see bad news as good news in disguise, and to take this as an occasion to understand his organization better, chiefly to identify what had gone so wrong that two-thirds of the staff rose up in open revolt. "I've seen and heard of other organizations that go through this four or five times," Hammond says. "I try not to make the same mistakes again, and I said, 'I've got a lot of strengths, but I also have a lot of weaknesses. And if I don't focus on those weaknesses, I'm never going to conquer them.'"

Hammond took the occasion to consider those questions and acknowledge that the answers had largely to do with him. With all his trips around the country, he had been inattentive, and the staff rightly felt neglected. And, in the early years of the organization's development, he should have offered more guidance. Further, he faulted his own management style and his way of addressing staff failures, which turned the staff against him. He realized that taking an erring staffer into his office for a lecture on what the person did wrong, and having him spread the word out to the rest of the staff wasn't the best way to handle problems. Finally, the incident revealed to him how fragile the organization was, as it still depended on him in nearly all areas of its operation, not just in terms of revenue, where he had placed so much of his emphasis. "I needed to be much more of a multitasker," he concludes. Still, the event was staggering, and it took both Hammond and KaBOOM! a good six months to recover. "The guy had full intentions of moving into my office!" Hammond says, still shocked. "Let's just say KaBOOM! wasn't a fun place to be for a while."

Managing the Business Your Start-up Has Become

There is something about gleaming new operations that seem to invite a monkey wrench to gum them up. They are audacious but understaffed, with grand plans but shaky financing. But the most important element is that they are new. They are organizations that are as new to their creators as they are to their stakeholders, and they are doing something new in a new way. All of this breeds vulnerability, as Hammond discovered. One key issue is, Who owns this new thing that seems to have come out of nowhere? In Hammond's case, his managing director felt that he owned KaBOOM! as much as Hammond did, even though Hammond had founded it. Actually, of course, neither one of them owned it. For a nonprofit is actually owned by the community it serves, and that community's representatives are the board of trustees, which is why at KaBOOM! it was up to the board to decide if Hammond was to stay or go.

That said, Machiavelli's rebellion was not entirely delusional. Sure, on the for-profit side, it is unimaginable that a senior vice president would try to take down the CEO and chairman of the board. But for corporations, ownership is purely financial, unlike the nebulous legal obligations that tie a nonprofit together. In the nonprofit realm, "ownership" is hard to define: no price is set and no shares awarded. It is one thing to say, airily, that a nonprofit is owned by the community it serves, but the members of that community aren't anything like the stockholders who own a public company. So our Machiavelli could indeed at least claim that he better reflected the purpose of the organization and thus was better suited to guide KaBOOM! than its founder. It was up to the board to determine that he was not.

Of course, one lesson that Hammond must have taken away from this was the same one that dictators already know: the wise leader stocks the board with loyalists he can count on when things get sticky. Ultimately, that is the only way to put down a coup—or keep one from being instigated. Yes, such blind loyalty can come at the cost of some independent thinking on the board, but there is no reason why such thinking shouldn't be tempered by a loyalty, if not to the founder himself then to his vision of where the organization should go. That is the most likely way to ensure that the nonprofit will realize that vision, and that the founder will be there to see it.

Although a coup may be one of the most dramatic crises that a young founder can face, it is by no means the only one. For the organization is headed into uncharted waters, with limited visibility and a rocky shoreline. If you're a founder, though, you'll

139

face as many internal hazards as external ones. Once you get deeply into it, you may find that it is all too much, too fractious, too frustrating, too uncertain, too crazy.

Or it's just *not you*. It was at the beginning, when your nonprofit was small and you could get your arms around everything and control it. But you may feel that your organization has evolved into something that doesn't suit you anymore. The style of it is off somehow, or the image. Maybe it's going too fast for you or is too much in the public eye or has turned corporate. It burns too much money, demands too much travel. All the entrepreneurs in our sample felt at least a twinge of regret when their enterprise took off. Their baby grew up! It got big, turned complex, and outgrew its tight, nurturing family to lumber out into the world.

Of course, a nonprofit grows up only because you let it. You can keep your operation small; you shouldn't feel any obligation to grow. One of our eighteen social entrepreneurs, Deborah Kenny, started a charter school in East Harlem, and by 2011, after considerable soul-searching, had added only four more. She is reluctant to expand further because she feels that she can have more impact by helping thousands of others learn how to run a good school than by opening a few dozen herself.

The truth is, founders often imagine that the little operations they started will stay little. But they rarely do. Although you don't absolutely have to grow—unlike a corporation that assumes it has to grow or die—nonprofits tend to, as most things in life tend to. Early on, in that cozy stage, you can, as we said, get your arms around the operation. There are just a few staff members and a few dozen clients, few enough that the staff are all good friends and the clients close acquaintances. But then the few staff members turn into quite a larger number; the client roster grows commensurately; you need a bigger office, more money, extra technology, finance people and techies to keep it all straight; and it all seems . . . different.

It's not a family anymore, but a business. And as the operation grows like a great oak, it pushes you, as the CEO, up and up to a height where you might not have wanted to go. You get the feeling that the organization is not just bigger than you but separate from you. It is much harder to manage from a height than from ground level. And, oddly, this feeling may not reinforce your pride in this achievement but detach your pride from it. It's not all about you anymore.

This can trouble you as a social entrepreneur. You might want to scale up because that feels like success, but then, when you do, you might feel that you've lost that lovely intimacy you had in the early days when it was just you and a very few others.

You know that the founder misses that spirit of the early days when she quietly goes back to doing those hands-on tasks she used to do when things were simpler. It's touching, like a grown-up going back to sleep in the bedroom of his childhood. For example, Jay Feinberg, of the blood and tissue bank the Gift of Life, makes a point of managing a few cases at any one time, just to keep his hand in and take part in the quest that drew him so intimately to the enterprise in the first place. Scott H. Silverman continues to work with a handful of cases, outside of Second Chance, to maintain the human contact he is missing as a chief executive.

Such activities arise from a useful kind of nostalgia, for they are reminders of what you find so meaningful about the work, and what sustains you still. It's a way of locating your bliss and keeping it. And that fundamental connection can be a good guide for your organization, too. You want to retain that hands-on intimacy for your own sake, sure, but also for the sake of your staff. It defines the essence of what you do, and of what your organization does. Be mindful of your passion, remember it, and keep it with you as you grow.

David Suzuki: When Things Get Out of Control

An attempted coup is certainly not the only difficulty you're likely to face as a founder in the early stages of your nonprofit's development. Lots of times, new founders discover cracks in what they'd always assumed was a unified operation, for there are plenty of potential structural flaws imbedded in a nonprofit from the very beginning. Oftentimes, they don't reveal themselves until the organization starts to grow, pushing the stresses of its early operation into view. If this is your nonprofit, you'll probably think, "How could I ever have missed that? How could I have been so stupid?" But the truth is, early on you didn't know what was going to matter.

David Suzuki should have seen it coming. He had agreed to give his name to a foundation with a loose purpose—"to protect nature"—indeterminate funding, no staff, and a structure that was split between the activists who had founded it and the as-yet-to-be-named fundraisers who were expected to find the resources for it. Somewhere along the way, it dawned on him that he and his wife, Dr. Tara Cullis, were supposed to run it, too. His dilemma was that he believed powerfully in the cause. Otherwise he would have walked away.

Infused with a sense of political outrage, having been interned with his family as Japanese Canadians during World War Two, he became a geneticist, and then was inspired by Rachel Carson to join the environmental movement. Emerging as a public figure, he started hosting *The Nature of Things,* a long-running environmental program on Canadian TV, in 1979. He also became a fierce environmental activist. He worked with the aboriginal people of the First Nations to protect their lands from logging and their waters from overfishing; protested a dam that was to be built on the Peace River; fought deep-ocean oil drilling; lobbied to halt nuclear tests in Alaska; turned some logging territory into a provincial park; and was part of a movement that supported indigenous people and eventually blocked a massive program of dam building on the Amazon's tributaries in Brazil. His efforts were not always warmly received. A bullet was once fired into a downstairs window of his house in Vancouver, presumably by an outraged logger. On another occasion, he was run off the road by a logger in a truck while jogging in Sandspit, a logging community in the Haida Gwaii islands of British Columbia.

In 1990, after completing a five-part radio series called *It's a Matter of Survival,* he became alarmed at the rate and extent of the ecological devastation throughout the world. The Worldwatch Institute, a highly regarded environmental think tank in the United States, warned that the 1990s should be defined as the "turnaround decade" to steer society away from its destructive path. To do something about it, Suzuki and his wife invited eleven environmental activists to a retreat on Pender Island in British Columbia, to discuss starting a new organization to address the issue. Somewhat naively, Suzuki never expected that the group would turn to him to be the leader.

Suzuki and Cullis established an organization with two arms, the foundation that would do the fundraising and an institute made up of environmental activists. The group did not say where the funds were to come from, but it had declared what money the foundation would *not* take—the government's, lest the group get hooked on it, or that of any corporations that weren't green. It took a year-and-a-half to develop the mission, and it ended up with a rather broad agenda, to put it mildly. "To protect nature, to protect ourselves," Suzuki says, by drawing on the best science to demonstrate nature's importance.

Before the fundraising arm could get going, Suzuki and Cullis began to give half their income to the cause. But their contributions, generous as they were, didn't go very far. "In the beginning, the money just got sucked into machinery and computers and faxes," he says. Obviously, they'd need more. So he became chief fundraiser, starting by turning to what was later dubbed his "platinum list" of individuals who had written in after *It's a Matter of Survival* was broadcast on CBC. He had received seventeen thousand letters, a tremendous outpouring, and most of them supportive of his efforts. Suzuki responded to each one of those letters as well as thousands of others written to him from his audience over the years, a kindness that proved providential. "Getting a handwritten reply turns out to be a very powerful way of getting a fan for life," Suzuki says, "one who will contribute." What Suzuki and Cullis had of a staff sent out solicitations for the new cause to as many of the fans as they could reach. "And money came pouring in," Suzuki recalls. "I mean, the postman came in with sacks of letters." Many of them bore checks. A direct-mail expert later told him that his return was ten times the normal rate.

But this wasn't purely good fortune, for it was a burden just to open so much mail and then to "receipt" the checks, accounting for them and sending out thank-you notes that matched the donations. And even though these donors might have contributed only $20 or $30, they would write back a few months later asking to know what had been done with their money.

It's unclear whether the money caused problems or revealed them. Either way, it is incontestable that the organization was worse off after it received the money, and so was Suzuki. Now that the foundation was in business, it was clear that no two people agreed on what it was supposed to do. "We had no idea what the hell we were doing," Suzuki laments. "I thought, the people that are involved in doing things, they're too busy to be involved in fundraising as well. So we'd better have a group that would raise their money, and they wouldn't have to worry about it." He pauses.

A new note comes into his voice. "Well, that was a fundamental error."

The operation fell apart almost immediately. The activists wanted to be active right away, he says. "They kept coming in and saying, 'Well, we want to get started on this program,' and they needed money. Well, it was coming out of my pocket. And very quickly it was way beyond anything that I could afford. But they weren't interested in waiting until we got the money. They were bugging us and harassing the volunteers and demanding that they go in and type and fax all these activities, because they didn't want to be bothered with that. They just wanted to get on and raise hell."

And the activists did all this completely on their own. "They would meet as a group, the Institute, and they would say, hey, we should do this, and we should do that. They were making the decisions, not me." He stops for a moment. "And so, yeah, it was stupid. It was really stupid on my part. There was a real tension between what we were trying to do to get this off the ground, and the activists. And that's when we thought, holy cow, we can't disengage the two. They've got to realize that their activities depend on our revenues."

It was around then that Suzuki and Cullis hit the wall. Suzuki says that Cullis bore far more of the organizational load than he did. She was the president, whereas he calls himself the "titular inspirer" and sometime chairman. Her health suffered tremendously as a result. "It was just such a pressure," Suzuki says. "There were several times when the activists were bugging us for money to get going, and I said, 'Tara, we can't do this. It's just too big for us. We can't do it. Let's drop it.'"

Eventually, in a tense conference call, the activists were made to realize that without Foundation funds, there really wasn't much for them to do except quit. And that is what they did. "They said,

'Well, really, there's not much reason for us to exist.'" With that they bowed out, eliciting nothing from Suzuki except a sigh of relief. That left the fundraising arm to serve as the entire entity.

Suzuki and Cullis then finally did what they should probably have done from the first: hire an executive director to run the operation, who left them to serve as de facto cochairs of the board, although Cullis retained her title of president and Suzuki gained a "phony-baloney" title of cofounder. The executive director, Jim Fulton, was well connected politically, having been a member of Parliament for fourteen years, but he also had good organizational instincts. He was the one finally to craft the mission statement, establish a working office, and chart a direction for the fledgling organization.

For the Suzuki Foundation's first project, Fulton decided to investigate the state of salmon in British Columbia. "We called in the experts and said, 'What are the problems? What's the good news?'" The foundation paid for a written report from salmon experts on the special perils of the fish, along with some proposed solutions, that won a fair amount of attention. That set the template for the foundation's work. It would apply the essential plan of "problem-solution, problem-solution" to a variety of ecological hotspots around the globe. The scientific reliability of the reports, the celebrity factor of the Suzuki name, and the seemingly free money of the go-go dot-com years—all served to swell the coffers of the foundation.

It got so that the organization expanded from ten people to forty, another bit of success that seemed to cause as many problems as it solved. "When you start developing larger numbers, you develop middle management, and then you see the human factors come into play. People get jealous. One person begins to think he's

146

more important than another person. You get cliques and factions and suspicions—all the human stuff." The foundation expanded from just the original office in Vancouver to four, adding French Quebec, Ottawa, and Toronto.

One of the new hires was a development director. She was needed because Suzuki was desperately tired of doing all the fundraising himself, "beating the bushes," as he says. It was so time consuming that it left him no time to get involved with designing the projects, which to him was the only fun part and, after all, the raison d'être of the foundation. It was the name again. "I kept telling people, look, you've got to wean yourself off the cult of my name." People kept turning to him for everything, to the detriment of the foundation as a whole.

Eventually the Suzuki Foundation stabilized, its goals clarified; its staff settled down. But its years of upheaval yield some important lessons for you as a founder, most of them having to do with the hazards of ambivalence about your role. Basically, you are either the founder or not. It is dangerously ambiguous for you to allow yourself to be perceived as the founder—meaning the one who has created the organization and bears the bulk of the responsibility for it—but not actually to be that in your own mind. At the very least, being seen as something you're not creates strain, but operationally it can be a disaster, as it nearly was for Suzuki. It left the CEO looking over his shoulder for a power figure who wasn't there, and left other members of the organization excessively deferential to Suzuki. He didn't just bear the name of the foundation; he also dispensed the money. The foundation was out of alignment, and the one who appeared to be in charge wasn't. If it weren't for the money that Suzuki was able to command, the foundation would likely have collapsed.

Getting Through the Hard Times

Difficulties are inevitable in the early going, when little is tied down and much shifts about. It is certainly helpful that all the staff be clear on the role they are to play, and that, of course, starts with the founder. Both Hammond and Suzuki struggled with this, Hammond because he was not hands-on enough with his staff and became out of touch with the mood of the organization, and Suzuki because he never really saw himself as the founder in the first place. But, beyond clarity of roles, a clear, universally accepted definition of the mission helps, too. For Suzuki, his own ambivalence mirrored uncertainty about the direction of the organization, and the combination was nearly ruinous. Clear leaders often dictate clear missions, and vice versa. If both are missing, look out—problems will inevitably arise, and they won't be small. But if you only have one, either a strong leader or a clear mission, that can usually be enough to pull an organization through the hard times. Still, it almost goes without saying that it is best to have both, and organizations that do are better equipped for the long haul.

CHAPTER 11

Preparing for Rollout

Ramping Up

WHAT DO YOU DO ONCE YOU'VE HONED your pitch, identified funders, and turned your idea into a reasonable proposition? In its fledgling stages, the operation is still mostly you, even though you may have brought in a staff member or two. Many organizations secure 501(c)(3) status, and if you do that you're required to have a board, but it would be wise to install one anyway. It may well be like Tommy Clark's, composed of family and friends, but the board members will help expand your expertise and contacts. In the best case, as with Mark Hanis and his dignitaries, they can do much more than that.

Through this seemingly endless developmental phase, the idea has always been your guiding light, and it remains your point of focus. Your goal still seems far away, however, and this makes for an anxious time. You have put in more money, time, and effort than you had ever imagined you would, and you have enlisted others to the cause as well. To the extent that this undertaking involves others, it becomes a greater worry. You don't want to let them down, but you don't want to lose control either. And there is the fear of the unknown. Maybe you will finally flip the switch on your new invention—and nothing happens. What then?

The point is that with any creation, from a new baby to a new novel, there is no predicting what will happen once it comes into the world. That is the nature, and thrill, of creating something. It's new, so there is no precedent to go by. Every act changes the world in some way, and rest assured that yours will, too. At the very least, it will change you, and it will probably change your clients. Whether the impact reaches beyond that to the wider world is largely a matter of luck, although careful planning can increase the chances that the luck will swing your way. At this point, all you can do is wait and see.

Sara M. Green: Going in Blind

Like all social entrepreneurs, Sara M. Green had no idea what to expect when the moment of truth arrived. She believed deeply in the value of bringing the arts to refugee camps. Would others? Would the refugees themselves? Green came to Art for Refugees in Transition (ART) obliquely. She'd been a professional dancer in France and the United States for ten years. To supplement her income, she'd done some fundraising and development work for various arts organizations and, in 1999, thought she might combine her passions and try to start a nonprofit. Under prodding from the Clinton administration, NATO had started bombing the Balkans, creating thousands of refugees. Green had visions of countless families pushing through the snowy mountains of Kosovo, some of the children hugging teddy bears. Green recalls,

> I was really struck by that, and I thought, those poor kids are going to Albania, and they've seen horrors we don't even want to think about—family members killed or raped right in front of them, horrible things that have taken away their childhoods, and things they can never get back.
>
> Probably it's just Western thinking, but many people have this idea that if something is wrong, you have to

150

talk about it. And here were these kids who have been through so much trauma, and they're going into a dark, cold, lonely place—literally—with nothing that reminds them of home, with traumatized family members as well. Wouldn't it be wonderful if there was an opportunity for them to express themselves? I've had difficult times in my life, everyone has, and people always say, "You need to talk to somebody. You need to talk it through." But I was a dancer, and I would always say, "I don't want to talk about it. Let me dance. Let me go to dance class. Let me go to rehearsal. Let me perform." Whatever it is, that would be my way of working through, working out, whatever was troubling me.

That perception started to lead her to ART, the work she does today. "I thought, wouldn't it be great if these children had a place where they could find themselves, where they could sing or dance or even just play and feel safe."

It wasn't until one night, though, that the full idea came to her. She woke up very early, and it was clear as anything. She actually said it out loud: "My God! I know what I want to do. I want to start arts programs in refugee camps."

She'd been in fundraising and development long enough to know that it would take more, and more from her, to bring her idea to fruition. She went to Columbia Business School for an MBA, learned many of the business skills she would need, and received a helpful credential as well. But she still worried, after all this, how the refugees would actually respond. There was no way to test the idea without actually doing it, and there was no way of doing it without getting her nonprofit going. It was largely to jump-start that process that she turned to the International Rescue Committee (IRC). ART would be a cultural offering that the IRC could add to the array of services it provided to the refugees. Green would train some of the IRC staff, who would in turn set up the program for the refugees themselves to run. It turned out that the IRC did work in a pair of Burmese refugee camps in Thailand, and Green began her work there. Her first visit was to a camp located deep in the rain forest on the Burmese border, forty-five minutes away from the nearest village. The camp itself dwarfed the tiny village in which it was located, a sprawl of ramshackle wooden homes, all of them up on stilts.

When Green arrived in the camp, she asked the IRC staff to assemble the elder refugees. They were the ones who would be best able to determine if the refugees would be interested in the program Green was offering, and whether it would work. Would anyone show up? Supposing she made this big offer of help, and no one took her up on it? "In my heart I knew it was right, and in my head, too," she says. "But practically?"

Her translator told her not to worry.

The announcement about the big meeting of the elders went out over the camp loudspeakers at top volume, in several Burmese dialects. At first the roads and alleyways were deserted, but then the elders started to emerge from their shelters, first in twos and threes and then by the dozen, and then more: hundreds and hundreds of them came out onto the street to make their way to the meeting place. When they were all assembled, Green managed to quiet everyone and, through her translator, described what she had in mind. She explained who she was and where she had come from, and then she asked, "Is it important for you to continue your cultural traditions? Your songs and dances and the other things you pass on to your children and grandchildren?" There was a general murmur, and people started shouting back, in Burmese, "Yes."

"And I asked, is this something you are doing now? And they said, 'No.' And I said, 'Is it something you want to do?' 'Yes, yes, yes.'"

With that, one woman started to sing, slowly and expressively. In that tribe, the Kareni, much of the history and tradition is passed down in song, and the translator explained that the woman was singing about how she missed her homeland and that she wanted to be back home. As she sang, many of the other elders gathered near her started to weep.

Then, suddenly, there was music, and Green looked up and saw some of the younger refugees emerge from the trees, loudly playing flutes and gongs, as if cued by the woman's song. And everywhere people rose up and started dancing wildly to the music. Recalls Green, "Everybody was crying, just crying and crying, hundreds and hundreds of people. And I had these goose bumps, and I was trying hard not to cry, just as I am trying hard not to cry now, thinking of it."

Puzzled, she asked one of the women why everyone had reacted like that. And she said that this was the first time since they had been in the camps—over fifteen years—that anyone had given them permission to feel. Sometimes the simplest spontaneous act provides people with the freedom to express themselves and their deepest feelings.

Doing Your Research, Then Deciding Whether to Listen to It

Uncertainty like Green's is fairly universal in nonprofits. Corporations may be able to pay for enough market research to give project managers a pretty good idea of what is going to happen, enabling them to prepare for it so that what happens next is more likely to go well. But such broad-based market research is beyond the reach of most nonprofits. For yours, you might consider a focus group, which is smaller, cheaper, and more manageable. For Green, even that would have been hard to pull off, but a directed conversation among a few stakeholders would have been within the realm of possibility. To the extent that it could have yielded key information about how her project might actually be received, such a conversation could have been a big help.

Still, test results are not to be confused with facts. They are just hypotheses that can be supported by research. And their predictive value is not all that high. There is a famous story, perhaps apocryphal, of a large electronics firm turning to a big-name consultant to test-market the idea of cell phones. After extensive research, the consultant issued a fat, handsome report which concluded that people basically had no interest in them: they'd much rather leave their telephones at home or in the office. One automaker got burned after it paid researchers to do blue-sky research about what kind of car people really wanted. The stated answer: a staid, boxy, safe vehicle that would get them reliably from point A to point B. So that is what the company produced, only to see cars remain glued to the showroom floor. Perhaps needless to say, consumers actually wanted something sexy; they were just too embarrassed to say so.

Still, if you turn to focus groups or other advisers, you should certainly listen; don't dismiss their ideas out of hand just because they conflict with your own suppositions. It is one thing to be committed to your idea, another to be blindly committed to it. To refuse counsel is to abandon the chance to learn. Sadly, this happens all the time: many social entrepreneurs will not hear a syllable of criticism about their baby.

In fact, it happened to us recently when a social entrepreneur approached us with an interesting idea about how to bring young people in to a stronger sense of community without exposing them to any of the off-putting aspects of ritual and organized religion. Curious about that ourselves, we were quite taken by the notion, and we offered to test his idea on a few younger, albeit highly experienced members of our staff who were close to his target market. They proved skeptical, but had some helpful observations that they wanted to pass along. When they did, the entrepreneur twice interrupted them and snapped at them defensively. Jeff couldn't believe it. "You came here to garner opinions of your product, and now you're lecturing us?" he asked. "You'd prefer to do that than listen?" The answer, alas, was yes. He'd put $200,000 into his project, and he wouldn't hear a negative word about it. He'd rather see it fail.

The Uncertainty of Rollout

That said, even if you have the most brilliant and attuned focus group in the world and you listen attentively to its responses, you still won't be able to take all that much of the uncertainty out of any rollout. The launch of any organization is rarely one great, smooth liftoff. You may have the funding, but implementation is flawed, or a myriad of other problems can keep you from getting things going. But no matter what, something is sure to go wrong, and probably many things.

Sometimes what seems like the perfect idea just sits there, possibly forever, because it has no way to get off the ground. We had an experience like that a few years ago for what was sure to be a brilliant program to take place in Africa: a service-learning program, meaning that young people would come together from various parts of the world to be trained in Israel to provide useful service in Central Africa. It was a terrific idea, a potential win-win-win, for the participants would learn about Africa, the Africans would benefit from their service, and Israel would enjoy some soft diplomacy. Everything came together—except the money. So the program has gone nowhere because it is waiting for someone to fund it.

One of our own signal programs, Birthright Israel—a program that takes Jewish students to Israel for ten days, all expenses paid—has been a spectacular success. But there were more than a few anxious moments for us as we waited for things to take off. Everything was all set, all the elements in place, except one. Were Jewish students actually going to apply? Either we got enough kids or we didn't. All or nothing. Yes or no. We had ample reason to be fearful. Marketing consultants had pointed out that few students, even Jewish students, were particularly interested in going to Israel. In fact, on the list of the countries our target population wanted to visit, Israel did not rank in the top twenty. But we tilted away from a connection to Israel that was based on guilt, and toward one that matched individual self-confidence to Israel's self-confidence. Because this idea was new, we didn't know how it would go down. So the day the applications were due, we were really nervous, pacing around our offices, waiting for the log-ons. The response was overwhelming. Birthright was a go.

Still, no such decision point is ever completely definitive; it just marks the first stage of the focusing process. You'll have to pass through many more stages before you reach that point called success. With Sara Green's ART project or our own Birthright, that first resounding yes from the marketplace was only the first, and there would have to be many more after that—from funders, from clients, from every conceivable stakeholder. The first yes establishes

156

the validity of the concept, but that's just where you start. There are no guarantees that the scheme will actually work over the long haul, let alone expand to the point of making a real difference in the world. It will need more money, much more, not just from a few friends and family but from independent donors; more staff, great hires, preferably; a talented, well-connected board; a deft but lean organization to handle all the complexity; brilliant strategic plans to take it to the next level; and marketing—on the cheap, of course—to get the word out.

The rollout will not be the calmest time for you. There is too much riding on it, and too much uncertainty to guarantee anything but sleepless nights. Careful, if not meticulous, planning will not remove all the uncertainty, not by a long shot, but it will improve your chances for success, and it will inspire you to focus on your concept as never before. This planning alone will yield insights, which may temper the impact of the market response among clients, funders, competitors, and the media. Once you are up and running, you will know far better what you are doing—and you can get started on the next phases of development.

PART THREE

Managing the Organization

"By God, gentlemen, I believe we've found it—the Fountain of Funding!"

CHAPTER 12

Becoming a Manager

The Change

FEW FOUNDERS START NONPROFITS WITH THE DREAM of someday managing them. For most, the transition just somehow happens. At first it's subtle, then it becomes more pronounced, and finally it is definitive. You're a manager. You might be called the managing director or the COO, but it is now your responsibility to run the organization, not just dream about it. This realization can come as a jolt. To most, that managerial role means difficult contract negotiations, personnel management issues, budget hassles, fundraising chores, and saying no. To many, the key difference between being a volunteer and being a nonprofit manager is that only the first one is fun.

The shift from entrepreneur to manager can be radical, as the two seem to occupy two opposite ends of the emotional spectrum. To wit:

- Entrepreneurs tend to be optimistic, sometimes wildly so. Managers have to be coolly realistic.
- Entrepreneurs believe in inspiration. Managers have to trust the process.
- Entrepreneurs freelance, dabbling in this and that. Managers depend on structure to keep everything organized and under control.

- Entrepreneurs are inclined to go it alone. Managers must mobilize a group.

They make an odd couple these two, especially when they are two sides of the same person.

That is not to say that you won't find any satisfaction in being a manager. First and foremost, being a manager is proof that your organization has officially come into being, which means you have survived. You have something to manage. That's an impressive achievement, and you should be proud of it. But the bottom line is, if you want to keep your operation going, you'll have to manage it or hire someone else to do it for you.

But beyond the thrill of survival, there is joy to be found as a newly minted manager. There is the pleasure of growing the operation, if you choose to take it to the next level, and then to the next one after that. Scaling up, either by expanding or going franchise, is exciting. In the nonprofit world no less than the for-profit one, many leaders believe that unless they are growing they are not fully alive. Which is to say, your career in advocacy isn't over; it has just changed.

Jay Feinberg: Making the Big Transition

Being a manager is different from being an advocate, no question, but that difference usually sneaks up on you. For Jay Feinberg of the Gift of Life, however, it struck the moment he received the bone marrow transplant that saved his life, since it called into question the purpose of the nonprofit he had created. "The question was whether we could continue to exploit the infrastructure we had created, the network of over a thousand volunteers we'd built, the knowledge we had amassed, and deliver all this for the benefit of

patients out there," he says. "Or whether we should close it down."
He pauses. "Well, for me it was a no-brainer." He had to keep
it going. But that meant, inevitably, that his role would shift. He
had been, uniquely, the subject and object of his nonprofit. Now
he would run it purely for the benefit of others.

If before it was something like a mom-and-pop shop, it now
had to grow into something closer to a serious business, one
that followed the normal rules of operation. And he would have to
manage it. "But it wasn't an overnight kind of thing, the switchover.
I didn't have my transplant and then say, you know, we're going to
set up the right board, and we're going to have committees, and we
have to have this person here for this department and that person
there for that department," says Feinberg. "It took time."

One reason the transition was not more dramatic was that it
was clear that the Gift of Life had to grow; the need was too great.
So Feinberg's role continued to have an entrepreneurial dimension.
He was always adding, innovating. He had always been on the
leading edge of donor search groups making use of the Internet,
which was a novelty when he started in the early 1990s. Was
this entrepreneurial or managerial? Well, it was both. Previously,
searches were all done manually, by looking through a file known as
the World Book published by an organization called Bone Marrow
Donors Worldwide. "It was literally a book that looked like the
Yellow Pages in the early days," Feinberg says. "Transplant centers
would take a ruler and go down the pages looking for a match."
In 1997, Feinberg went online with his donors so that patients
could run their searches in real time and get results right away.
Donors could also sign up on the Web to join the registry and
receive a kit mailed to their homes. Another innovation: instead
of drawing blood, which requires those stressful needle sticks, he
used cheek swabs. And he invested in the technology to do the
"full typing"—identifying the blood and tissue characteristics of

potential donors—at the place of recruitment, greatly increasing efficiency.

But as the Gift of Life grew, Feinberg could feel the tug of practicality, forcing him to attend to the existing operation in increasingly exacting ways. He thought of it as shifting his nonprofit from a family-and-friends basis to a professional one. "It wasn't easy, quite frankly," he begins. "It was an emotional transition, at least at the beginning. But I realized that if we didn't make that transition, we'd be stuck. We wouldn't be able to move to the next level."

The change manifested itself most profoundly on the board, which had been, as he says, "your typical founding board—family and friends." It consisted of his parents, primarily, and some family friends who had been helpful from the beginning. But he soon realized that he needed to branch out, to establish a board based on professional affiliations, in hopes that the specialized talents and social connections would stimulate the organization's growth.

Feinberg was starting to think like a manager. Conventionally, entrepreneurs are so busy growing their operations that they have no time to attend to the systems that sustain them. They're for managers to handle, and that's what Feinberg learned to do. Seeking new board members, he reached out to people who were attached to the cause because they were themselves transplant recipients, or they knew someone who needed a transplant. Such a visceral connection provided powerful emotional capital for Feinberg to draw on. But they also possessed the talents, connections, and money that the organization would need to establish itself.

Building the new board was not a speedy process, not by any means. "I didn't just come up with a list of high-profile people and ask them, 'Can you join my board?'" he says. "It took time." He sighs. "But the other thing is that it was important to me not to just tell the people who were our founding board members that they're no longer needed and that we've got to move on and ask them to leave. I wasn't prepared to do that."

But in making the shift gradually, Feinberg had to go through a long period during which the board was half fish, half fowl—neither a full family board nor a completely professional one. "It brought some complexity also with respect to what was expected of board members," he admits tactfully. "We went through that sort of mixed chimerical state where you had a combination of different players. But eventually the legacy board members did rotate off the board, and we were left with what we have today. But it took some time. It really did."

One reason it took so long was that he wasn't about to force any family members off the board, but had to wait until they left on their own. This revealed a manager's response to the issue—patient, cautious, but still focused. In the end, no feelings were hurt. "I think they left because they felt it was right, and they saw what they had built and the direction that we needed to go in."

That patience is telling. Entrepreneurs and managers have different senses of time. Entrepreneurs operate in a world where they don't think there is time for anything: the due date is always last week. The scramble over impossibly tight deadlines reflects the scramble for everything—money, manpower—to make anything happen at all. Result: a chaos that the entrepreneur hopes will be creative. For managers, however, time spools out to the horizon, not because they have so much of it, but because they need to take the long view, the better to prepare for the future. As they budget out their time, they budget other resources, intelligently allocating—in the best case—what is available to what is needed.

Feinberg also realized that he had to rearrange the organizational chart so that he wasn't responsible for everything, as he had been previously. He necessarily had to rise to the top of the pyramid, but in moving up, he had to let go of some of the more routine functions that he had either taken care of or overseen previously. It was not an easy adjustment. "I think the hardest thing for me has been accepting that I can't do everything," he says, "and that I have to delegate responsibility to the right people and take that burden off myself." He needed, he adds, to focus on "higher-level things." Fortunately, he trusted his colleagues at Gift of Life implicitly; many of them had worked for the organization since the beginning. The transition from entrepreneur to manager was an emotional as well as functional one. "I had to get over this thing where it's my baby, and not micromanage." Just recently, he says, he'd been out of the office entirely for a couple of weeks, as he flew about the country to meet with potential contributors, develop relationships with transplant centers, create partnerships with recruiting organizations, and perform other tasks that attend to the needs of the entire organization, now and in the future, that he had not possessed the head space for previously.

Settling into Management

In the entrepreneurial stage, you are creating an organization out of nothing. There is an inherent unpredictability to that, a vulnerability to circumstance. Critical factors—technological, logistical, financial—are likely to be beyond your control. When he started out, Darell Hammond had no idea that he would end up partnering with Home Depot. Carolyn LeCroy, of the Messages Project, didn't know that it would be so hard to get money. The start-up phase is bound to be a wild ride, and everyone needs to hang on tight.

As the organization settles down and turns to you to be more of a manager, the bumpiness should have eased off. Indeed, it is your job to find, and stay in, calmer air. Funding should be steadier, planning more predictable, and the organization more stable. A place where tomorrow isn't likely to be so different from today.

When we laid out the entrepreneurial phase of nonprofit development in this book, we set the chapters out chronologically, starting with that moment of inspiration and then moving through the early stages of growth after that. As you settle into being a manager, you'll find that one topic doesn't lead naturally to the next one in a chronological way. The sequence is likely to be far more random. At times, you'll probably feel as though you're always on defense as these different issues loom up unexpectedly. There are about a half-dozen topics that you are likely to face, and in the coming chapters we will address them the way they are likely to appear—randomly.

CHAPTER 13

The Board

How the Board Can Help

NO MANAGER OPERATES ALONE. THAT'S ONE REASON why there are boards of directors, and that's why Jay Feinberg paid such attention to his. In the best case, the directors are your guardian angels, providing what you need when you need it. Funds, connections, strategic advice, moral support—all of them should, ideally, be made available to you in a twinkling. In reality, board members are not angels, but they are, at least, in a position to offer essential help, and usually of a mind to at least try to provide it. This is why the IRS is probably wise to require them as a condition of awarding 501(c)(3) nonprofit tax status.

It can get a little lonely at the top, and a manager who is new to his position can use all the support he can get. Staff members can provide sound suggestions, but as a manager you always have to consider the source, and you might wonder if their advice is self-serving or politically inspired. Informal advisers outside the organization might be helpful, but they don't often know the facts on the ground. The board, however, is perfectly placed to know the basics, but not so close as to be prejudiced, and it can bring fresh insight to the issues at hand. The board is designed to be the steward of the organization's future. That's the theory, anyway.

Darell Hammond: A Board of Heavy Hitters

Darell Hammond's management team at KaBOOM! was drawn from the ranks of Fortune 500 companies. The board itself is drawn from a wider range of backgrounds that are possibly more impressive, as the members range from the CEO of New Balance, the director of policy and governmental affairs at the Gates Foundation, a franchisee of a Curves women's fitness center, and a professor and self-described "chief curator and provocateur" at the global marketing consultancy Prophet. For Hammond, the board serves as the standard to which he is aspiring with his organization, and it is one that he, about two decades younger than the average age of his board members, is showing considerable pluck to shoot for. To him, the board is less a trampoline that is launching him higher and more a magnet, pulling him up to a higher level and holding him there. "Our board chair is the former CFO of a Fortune 500 company, and our board vice chair is the CEO of a $1.6 billion privately held company," Hammond says, "and they'll tell you that our management team and our financials and our strategy projections and formulation are as good as their own businesses and the boards they sit on in the corporate world." But they provide more than just a measure of success. They also provide the standard of it. And for a new nonprofit with a young CEO, the combination has created a powerful basis for success. "When you're doing business with business, you've got to talk the walk with them. You have to differentiate yourself by the essence and the spirit and the passion and the execution of the endeavor. I have seen and heard people who can talk a really good business plan in the nonprofit sector, but can't execute it. And I've seen people who can execute well but can't fulfill the business model. They can put the output and the incomes in alignment so the thing makes sense financially." To the extent that KaBOOM! has achieved that balance of doing nonprofit work with for-profit partners, Hammond believes he has his board to thank. Then again, he was the one to dare to think big in the first place, to select them and persuade them to join up. This is how successful managers think, and what they do.

Scott H. Silverman: The Burden of Too Much Advice

Whereas the board for KaBOOM! has provided insightful advice and useful guidance, there is always a countercase—the board that dispenses advice freely but lacks the feel for the organization that would make that advice worth hearing, let alone acting on.

Rather than rely on national figures, Silverman stocked his board at Second Chance with a standard array of local committed San Diegans, most of them lawyers, bankers, and real estate people, but few of them with a deep stake in the success of the organization. They were selected by the board's nominating committee, with input from Silverman and the founding members. If Hammond feels nothing but gratitude for the help and inspiration offered by his board, Silverman often found himself frustrated by an imbalance between give and take at the board meetings. In his view, too often, they gave and he had to take—regardless of the pertinence or value of the advice. He wasn't convinced that a board of corporate-minded outsiders can ever really *get* a unique nonprofit operation. "I think board members tend to hang their business hat on the wall when they walk into a board meeting," says Silverman.

And the things they might ask of leadership in a nonprofit they probably never would ask of their own business. Here they are, they're coming as a volunteer and they have a role as the chair of a finance committee, or of the development committee, or of strategic planning, or of anything. And you're an executive director or CEO, and you've got this operational responsibility, and they'll come up with "Hey, why don't you try doing this?" Because that's something they might do in their business. And they don't think it through like they would in their business, to set up a strategic plan. It's well intended—to help the agency get resources or help people—but it comes across as impulsive. It's like they're starting a new business every time they do that. It's not mean or malicious, but it's not thought through. And from what I hear, it's happening to nonprofits more and more with strategic planning, and the EDs or the CEOs say, "Hey, you can't just change what you do in twelve months of strategic planning if you've been doing it for five, ten, fifteen, twenty years."

And it got worse. Some of these questions weren't limited just to strategic planning, but to the very purpose of the organization. "Every organization has its mission statement and its vision statement," Silverman says. To him, they are sacrosanct, like the Ten Commandments or the Bill of Rights. But to board members who are not versed in the fundamental procedures of a nonprofit, they are open to revision. "'Hey people,' they might say. 'It's time to update the mission.' Well, to me that's like, are you kidding me? That's like reinventing the whole environment."

To Silverman, the essential problem in the nonprofit arena is that neither side of the equation—neither the leader nor the board—is fully equipped for the role it plays. Entrepreneurial nonprofit leaders are rarely professionally trained, but have essentially put themselves in their positions. And board members rarely know enough about how nonprofits operate, or even how boards operate, to make seasoned judgments. To Silverman, it's the blind leading the blind. So what's the answer? To Silverman, it's time—time to gain what he terms "alignment" between the leadership and the board, so that each understands the other and can work together. As it was, though, his board chairman's two-year term was likely to expire before that alignment was found, the slate changed, and Silverman had to start all over. It's like the federal government, he concludes. Every two or four years it turns over in a dramatic fashion. "And not a whole lot gets done."

Given the sharp division between him and his board, and his intractable attitude, it will not come as a huge surprise that he and the board ultimately decided to separate, with Silverman leaving the organization he founded. It was not a pretty result, but it was probably an inevitable one. In such situations, the leader, even if he is also the founder, has to recognize that the organization is not his to rule, no matter how integral his role. Actually, it is not the board's either. As we mentioned earlier, a nonprofit is owned by the community it serves, and the board serves as a representative of its interests. As such, it will always be the one to decide if the leader stays or goes, and, to Silverman's frustration, it did.

What Makes a Good Board

There are different methods of choosing board members, but most nonprofit boards are selected by some version of a nominating committee that selects members and submits them to the full board for formal approval. Nowadays, it is not uncommon to use headhunters to find the perfect board member for an available slot, but such searches are expensive and definitely not for everyone. As the founder, you would certainly be given leeway to propose your own choices, and the nominating committee would almost certainly go along. To the extent that such personal connections foster collegiality, their inclusion is all to the good. Boards need a relaxed atmosphere in order to foster a full and free exchange. But you might be wise *not* to try to pack the board with your selections, or you will close off the independent perspective that can broaden an organization's horizons.

Board members should be conscientious, reading all the materials before each meeting and showing up reliably. They are expected to take an independent view, but an informed one. Here the selection of the chair can be key, as his or her behavior will serve as the model for everyone else's.

It's instructive that the money flow triggers the 501(c)(3) nonprofit status that leads to the creation of a board. There is no question that one of the board's critical functions is to help assure that flow, by governing, contributing, soliciting, reviewing and approving budgets, and overseeing key policies. (One adage about board service refers to the "three G's": the board member's job is to "give, get, or get off.")

Too often, board members miss the essential fact that they don't own the nonprofit, but are merely stewards of it for the community. It means they should take their work extremely seriously by attending board meetings, studying board materials, and setting aside personal considerations to deliver thoughtful decisions on matters of policy. They should ask probing questions of the staff, and not be ashamed to seek out more information if necessary. By the same token, the staff should be diligent about providing the structure conducive to the board's doing its best work: written agendas that lay out the strategic and policy issues under discussion; educational materials; an atmosphere conducive to informed, purposeful discussion; a committee structure; and encouragement for board members to contribute to the organization in other ways.

In seeking out volunteer board members, we like "the five W's," those attributes that will likely result in a higher-functioning board: wealth, wisdom, work, wit, and wallop.

Which is the greatest of these? Given the requirements of the money flow, you might think wealth, and, without question, funds are essential to the operation of any nonprofit. But wealth will do you no good without generosity. So we'd pick wisdom, if we can define it as being wise in the ways of the world.

Probably you want your board member to be influential, but how influential? Is a national reach important, or merely a local one? Winning a celebrity board member who is much in demand can be exhilarating—until you discover that he or she has no time left to give you. Is your candidate clubbable? Like it or not, a board has some of the characteristics of a private club—exclusivity, insularity. Everybody needs to get along with everybody, so it is best not just to rely on resumes or a sparkling endorsement but to try out the chemistry at a social event before bringing the person on for a three-year term.

By the same score, it is important that all the board members contribute to the cause every year, no matter how little. It demonstrates buy-in, and potential donors will want to see a high contribution rate from the board. Racial, ethnic, and gender diversity on the board is important. Your board's diversity should mirror that of your community and of your potential clientele. In general temperament, you want a board that is thoughtful, and able to give deep and ample consideration to the organization's work and methods. It can show appreciation for the things that have gone right, and, as for the things that may have gone wrong, give suggestions that are respectful of the leadership, positive minded, realistic, clear, and doable. And a sense of humor can be essential to get through those inevitable rough patches in board life.

Boards should appreciate that they are policymakers, not operational in their outlook. If a board spends more time on "administrivia" than on policy, serious problems will follow. This respectful understanding is the quality that should bridge the divisions between board and leadership that Silverman spoke of. The board should be able to see things from your perspective as well as its own. Ideally, there should be a member or two who are closely involved in the area of the nonprofit's work. If the nonprofit deals with issues of children with disabilities, then it would be helpful to have a parent of a disabled child, or perhaps an adult who has had a disability from childhood, on the board to offer a consumer perspective. Feinberg used this approach at the Gift of Life, recruiting board members personally affected by the need for bone marrow transplant. Again, you certainly want a board that reflects the population being served, not just the one doing the serving.

Certain professions are immensely helpful on a board, primarily business, law, and accounting. These professionals might be cajoled into providing some of their services for free. What the board as a whole does, or can be expected to do, depends on where it is in the life cycle of the nonprofit. Initially, they are presumably available for everything from finding donors to giving hands-on help. As the board develops, it has an increasing responsibility for setting policy, although it would certainly do this in close communication with you as the founder.

In general, though, you should proceed on the assumption that each member of the board is there because he or she adds value, so the sensible thing to do is to exploit that value. (On a pro bono basis, of course. You don't want any of the ethical conflicts on the board that would result from putting money on the table.) Their skills can come in very handy. Suppose you want to create a play street. It would be a big help to have a local zoning lawyer and someone who is politically connected, or maybe a former police officer, who might be able to put in a good word at the local precinct.

How Boards Work

Who runs the meeting? If you, as the founder, remain unpaid and serve on the board, you might. If you take a salary and serve as executive director, you should cede that role to the (unpaid) chairman of the board.

The United Way developed helpful language in this regard, as it distinguished between the chief volunteer officer and the chief professional officer. It's the chief volunteer officer who chairs the meetings. Customarily, a board meets as often as necessary to fulfill its mandate, with various subcommittees—nominating, finance, and the like—meeting more frequently than that. But as the founder, you should feel free to call members up at other times if you have a question or a request. They are there to help, and if they won't help, they shouldn't be there. Whether you direct the meetings or not, you should rely on your board. You want to draw out of it what you need. Whether you, as founder, serve as chief volunteer or chief professional, you get out of your board no more than you put in. Engagement is key. Think strategically, focus on what you are trying to accomplish, and find board members who can help you get things done.

CHAPTER 14

Transparency

No Secrets

MANY OF THE PRINCIPLES OF MANAGEMENT are age-old; they may seem like basic common sense. But some are fairly new to the scene and may take some getting used to. We are thinking primarily of the need for transparency, which has become a management buzzword of late, partly due to the rise of the Internet and social media. To be transparent is not human nature. Individuals are inclined to draw the living room drapes and to keep their cards close to their vest. To go public, after all, is to invite public commentary, which can bring disagreement. For a manager to keep secrets, though, will only invite trouble.

To understand the necessity for something that can be so onerous, we first need to revisit an important principle, the one that makes it clear that your nonprofit really isn't yours at all. It is the community's. It has been your good fortune to be able to create an institution that meets the IRS requirements to become an official 501(c)(3)–designated nonprofit. This requires a board of directors, a limitation on salaries, and a returning of any "profits" to the organization as investment capital. These requirements reflect the essential and distinctive characteristic of nonprofits, that they exist to benefit the community and not to enrich their creators. Nonprofit status allows the organization to avoid taxes and allows donors to take a tax deduction for their contribution. That, in turn, forces you to be accountable because you are acting in the public trust. Why else would the tax man forgo all those taxes?

One other big reason for transparency is that you can't possibly avoid it. Nowadays, in the Internet era, a nonprofit is a glass house, and everyone can see what you do whether you want to show people or not. Online services like Charity Navigator will rate your efficiency—the value of your service divided by the cost of producing it—on every conceivable metric. It's a bit like *U.S. News & World Report*'s annual college rankings. Charity Navigator rates your efficiency by gathering up all the public information about your operation, which is much more than you'd think, sets it out in comparison to a host of other social enterprises in your category, and publishes the results on the Web for all to see. Soon it will be introducing other measures of your effectiveness, too. Interestingly, this is philanthropy at work on philanthropy. Disruptive philanthropy, to be more precise. And it has done more to haul philanthropy into the modern age than any other recent initiative. Millions of new donors, when they are hurriedly considering making a gift between Thanksgiving and Christmas, as many of them do, turn first to Charity Navigator and decide on their gift based on the number of stars a charity has received. Most social leaders have not caught up to the fact that Web sites like this will help determine their future—and they need to.

Again, nonprofits are not like for-profits. Nonprofits are subject to more public scrutiny than most for-profit companies. On the for-profit side, much information is proprietary, as it concerns matters relevant to corporate advantage. On the nonprofit side, with precious few exceptions, such as preserving secrets regarding any scientific research, it is all in the public domain. The work of nonprofits is assumed to be advancing society. After all, you're supposed to be doing good. And if you are—say, by providing a new way for prisoners to communicate with their families, and thus lowering prison recidivism—you should not keep the good news under your hat.

How Transparency Works

Most of the major structural elements of a nonprofit are on public view. Nonprofit tax forms are available on GuideStar, another guide to nonprofits, and those forms in turn reveal annual revenues and expenses in considerable detail, similar to an individual's 1040. Even the salaries of the top five officers are on view. Many nonprofits, in the interests of transparency, also put their 990 tax return on their Web site. How far to go with this can be a tough call for managers, and larger operations often have chief compliance officers to handle these issues. Their job, however, is not only to follow the rules and regulations of the field of operation but also to observe the highest ethical standards. The rules and regulations are precisely defined; you are either in accordance or you're not. Ethics are more subjective, but certain professionals develop a sense of what kinds of behavior are expected. Even if you can't afford to hire a dedicated compliance officer, you can certainly enlist a lawyer for your board who can make a dispassionate judgment about some trying issue should one arise. If, for example, a vendor wants to fly you out to speak at a winter conference in Palm Springs when your office is in Bangor, Maine—is that okay? It comes down to whether the vendor wants you for your expertise (okay)—or for your business (not okay). That is hard to decide in freezing Bangor, when sunny Palm Springs looms. That is what a compliance officer or an objective trustee is for. Although the facts are certainly important, the appearances are possibly even more so. Just a few whispers about impropriety, and a fledgling nonprofit can easily be damaged and possibly doomed.

Although individual decisions can be pivotal, the larger issue is one of attitude, of mind-set. The fact is, nonprofits need to operate on a radically different basis from many for-profits. This need for heightened transparency is another place where, for a manager, everything starts to interconnect with everything else. For example, hiring decisions are also transparency issues. Not so much because you're obliged as a manager to be open about the hiring process. You're not. But you should hire employees who understand the need for transparency and will transmit it through the ranks. In this effort, a compliance officer can be helpful not just to make the tough ethical calls but also to stand for the importance of making them. At for-profits, the desire for transparency is often a showy extra, something to display more than to employ. At the best nonprofits, that inclination is built right in, affecting the way everyone does their work.

In general, the public's increasing insistence on transparency has improved the conduct of nonprofits: any skullduggery has become that much harder to conceal. In the shadows of American corporations, corruption is much easier to pull off. It is restrained largely by individuals' morality, which is not always sufficient to the task. (In one story making the rounds: an executive was asked to lower his valuation of his company, one a larger firm was set to acquire. If he did, he would be asked to stay on as head of that division and get a $1 million bonus besides. He said no, which is why he tells the story, but he has no doubt that others would say yes.) Scandal operates in the dark; transparency provides light. The tragedy is that when a nonprofit employee engages in nefarious behavior, he hampers the organization's ability to do its work—and damages the public trust in the whole nonprofit enterprise.

Standards of compensation for the senior executives is another serious board responsibility, surrounded by human resource, regulatory, public relations, and ethical considerations. There are many resources available to assist boards in creating appropriate compensation policies. It is critical that stakeholders understand the variables and that there be clear communication surrounding these issues.

CHAPTER 15

Planning for the Future

What to Do Next

YOUR ORGANIZATION HAS MET ITS INITIAL GOALS. You've gotten it off the ground. Maybe things are moving forward apace, or maybe things are starting to flounder a bit. Or perhaps you've plateaued, and although the organization isn't in crisis, it is in need of a boost and some direction. This point in its life cycle presents a great opportunity to do what you probably should be doing regardless of how well things are progressing: engaging in strategic planning. This is how organizations develop and solidify, as opposed to retreating and losing focus.

It's time to take stock of your situation and decide what's next. Are you growing too quickly to keep up? Or if you're not growing quickly enough, should you be developing a growth plan? Are you accomplishing what you set out to do? Are you measuring your outcomes? To plan for the future, you need a full understanding of where you are at present. Ideally, strategic planning can not only generate an action plan for the future but also develop a refreshed and invigorating sense of consensus across the various stakeholders of the organization, and pump up the whole organization, providing focus, alignment, and cranked-up intensity. To accomplish all of this, crisis, paradoxically, offers the best opportunity, as everyone is forced to recognize that something *has* to be done. But a pervasive sense of need—even without a

185

crisis—should be enough to get buy-in from all the stakeholders so that they'll participate in the process and endorse the results.

As a first timer, you may be tempted to conduct the strategic analysis yourself, as it would save you a fair amount of money. But you're a manager now. You need to remember that there are other people in your organization, so the wisest course of action is to consult with your board. Depending on the makeup of your board, it may be able to give you direction or may decide to turn to a local professional consultant. Unlike you, a consultant is in the position to solicit candid answers from a wide variety of stakeholders, perform the appropriate analysis, develop a plan, and present it to the board to act on.

Conducting a SWOT Analysis

Usually, consultants will begin by determining the basic GPS coordinates of the organization—where it is in the competitive landscape—then use their findings to suggest where it should go and how to get there. To do this, they use an assessment rubric called SWOT—for *strengths, weaknesses, opportunities,* and *threats,* the core elements that reveal the organization's status and potential.

Again, it is important to emphasize that the direction the organization always needs to be traveling in is the one that leads toward ever greater fulfillment of its mission. As you remember from that taxonomic ranking of the levels of organizational purpose, the one that runs from mission on down to measurement, the core idea of any organization has to be its mission. Any strategic plan has to reflect that on every page. The strategy within the strategic plan is one that will best make the mission happen. To veer off in another direction, without the approval of the board, will lead to all sorts of identity issues and will require such massive retooling that it would amount to the creation of a completely new organization. This is what Scott H. Silverman was thinking of when he complained about board members who blithely recommended massive reconceptualizations of his Second Chance, without any regard to its history or trajectory.

Presumably, the mission of your organization was set down early. That would immediately lend focus to your consultant's work. Gathering more general information about the potential market would also be important. Depending on the nature of your organization, this may mean doing some demographic surveys and examining opportunities. Doing some geographical analysis in order to see if there are some seriously underserved areas might also be helpful.

Even when the questions are honed, such an investigation is likely to yield statistics galore. The issue is to find the data that can actually lead to a strategic decision and then to convince the deciders to rely on those data to decide. That sounds obvious, but far too often these strategic reports end up on a shelf somewhere gathering dust. One way for you to make sure they mean something is to develop a point of engagement with the board from the outset. This is commonly done through a separate strategic planning committee made up of key board members. If your board is small, you may not have all that many members to pick from, but larger organizations that do should assign their heavyweights on the board to that committee assignment. In sheer practical terms, because those members are likely to be the most prominent, their commitment will encourage others to take strategic planning seriously as well. Their presence signals importance.

The committee also gives the board a chance to provide some monitoring and guidance. And, having done that, the board then will need to take responsibility for the outcome. To the extent that the consultant is left to wander off with his notebook, unsupervised, the final product is likely to remain unclaimed, a dead letter that is forgotten moments after it is presented. But if there is active engagement, then the process offers a rare chance for the whole organization—not just the board but every constituency all the way around—to reengage, and to revivify itself. At the very least, taking part in such an analysis will send a message that the organization is determined to move forward, and at the very most, the organization will receive information and buy-in from its stakeholders that will enable it to do just that.

But bringing in a professional consultant isn't the only way to move forward. Truth be told, among the eighteen social entrepreneurs whom we interviewed, only a few have used consultants for strategic advice, although many wish they had. They've tended to rely more on their own instincts as to how to proceed, and to be leery of an expensive report from some professional. In this, they may be thinking of themselves too much as seat-of-the-pants entrepreneurs who make things up as they go. We are thinking of Milo Cutter, who, when trying to make important decisions about her school, relied on her most crucial stakeholders, the students, as focus group members and strategists, and consciously developed her charter school on the basis of what they "wanted it to look like." Or Sara Green, who had no idea if her plan to bring arts programs to refugees would have any appeal until she tested it out on the refugees themselves. This is how entrepreneurs operate. But managers are different. When they face a profound decision about the future of their organization, they are indeed likely to turn to a strategic consultant to help them frame the issue in a manner conducive to making the most sensible decision. Such was the case of City Year's Michael Brown when he was deciding how to grow his organization.

The Two Paths to Growth

As we've said before, the desire to grow is not universal, nor should it be, but it is common, and there are basically two modes of accomplishing it. One is by expanding the central office, so that it can run a larger operation. This is the model for most corporations, who maintain a large headquarters by which they run an expanding number of satellite offices spread over an ever wider geographical area. Rebecca Onie's Health Leads has done this, expanding from its original site in Boston to five additional cities. It has staffed up accordingly and changed its name to Health Leads to reflect its expanded reach. Anne Heyman is contemplating something similar, as she ponders duplicating her Rwanda project in Haiti. Her employees are project based, not operation based, so the integration problems there are not so pronounced, but still such a change would double the size of her organization. By growing in a centralized fashion, these social entrepreneurs are staying true to the spirit that inspired them originally, as a centralized operation can grow somewhat impetuously, adding dimension when the founder sees fit. Also, it allows the founder to keep hold of the entire entity, as he would govern from a central location, with all branches reporting to him.

But there are liabilities. The larger an organization gets, the more complex it becomes. Instead of having one vice president, or two, the CEO soon has six or eight, and they are all jockeying for power, seeking to place their stamp on the nonprofit as a whole. As at the top, so below. The number of employees is likely to grow dramatically, giving rise to a host of potential interpersonal problems and turf battles. The operation will become more expensive, requiring more fundraising. As it expands into more states in distant parts of the country, there are also more regulatory and legal issues that need to be addressed.

By contrast, there is the franchise model—McDonald's, KFC, Dunkin Donuts. The for-profit landscape is filled with them, and they serve as models for the nonprofit side as well. Like commercial franchises, nonprofit franchises are, ideally, exact replications of the original enterprise. Xerox copies. Robert Carmona, for example, is growing STRIVE not by expanding his own organization but by supporting franchises in other states. One of the first, of course, went to Scott H. Silverman.

These can be attractive because they are hand-offs. You as the founder hand off the rights to building a nonprofit shop exactly like the one you started in Baltimore, and someone else will build one in San Diego or Austin. The good part is that the franchisees do it; you as the founder don't, so it is a way to grow dramatically and relatively painlessly. This is also the bad part, for there is a natural tendency of any franchisee to veer off the founder's path and onto her own. So great care has to be taken to ensure that franchises indeed all stay the same. The franchisor will have to create a book of standards, a kind of pattern book that exactly describes what a franchise is supposed to be. It would cover everything from the color and typeface of the logo to the content of the work. Commercial franchises have them, and they are exacting, which is why a McDonald's in Beijing looks like one in Newton, Massachusetts. To make sure franchisees stick to the script, many franchisors end up sending the nonprofit equivalent of "secret shoppers" to check a franchise mental health facility, for example—to see what the waiting room looks like, experience the care, get a sense of the schedule.

Which of these two approaches to growth is better? Much depends on the style of the leader. If you are the hands-on type and have boundless energy for dealing with a growing organization, then you should probably centralize if you want to grow. Otherwise, you'd be better off franchising, as that transfers many of the headaches to others. Of the two styles, the franchise model is substantially more popular, probably for that reason.

Michael Brown: Deciding How to Grow City Year

Michael Brown's City Year, the organization that brings young people, generally for the year between high school and college, into American cities to provide mentoring and guidance to struggling younger students, had to choose one of these two paths. After starting in Boston and growing the organization there, Brown went through an elaborate procedure in deciding how to ramp it up. It became increasingly tempting to go national after then Governor Bill Clinton caught on to it during the 1991 presidential campaign. Shortly before the New Hampshire primary, Clinton sat with a group of City Year volunteers, who impressed him so much that when one literally gave him the City Year T-shirt off his back, Clinton wore it frequently as he jogged during his presidency.

City Year sparked the idea of a federally funded AmeriCorps, a kind of domestic Peace Corps funding bank, which in turn provided as much as a half of City Year's budget. For some time, other cities had been clamoring for a City Year operation of their own, and in 1993, now with money more secure, Brown's partner Alan Khazei thought it was time to grow beyond Boston. Brown was dubious, remembering that City Year was intended only as a demonstration project for the idea of national service. But, with AmeriCorps, that work was essentially done. Unlike the Peace Corps, AmeriCorps was solely a funding source, and what it needed was programs.

The question then became *how* to take this national. Should it be in a centralized way, with a national headquarters and satellite branches in a hub-and-spoke model? Or through licensed franchises? And if they were to be franchises, what kind should they be? "And that's where we stepped back and said, 'We need some strategic planning.'" The questions were legion. "This was a phase change for the organization, like it was shifting from a liquid to a gas. It was a whole new period. And it required some very big decisions. Like—would it be one company? Would it be separately incorporated? Would these be local boards that are fiduciary boards using our name under some kind of charter? Or what?"

Brown and Khazei had a friend, Roger King, a consultant with Bain and Company at the time, and he agreed to do the strategic work on the key question of whether to stay with one company or split into several independent ones. King ran through the analysis, pointing out that most nonprofits—the Red Cross, the YMCA, the Boys and Girls Clubs—ended up taking the latter route, "separately incorporated with local fiduciary boards," Brown says, "using a brand name that everybody bought into." Franchises, in short. King also raised the standard caveats—that each local City Year might develop independently from the central one and from all the others, and the central one would have little control over the strategic direction of the locals. He noted, however, that the franchise approach allows for much quicker and greater proliferation. If expansion is directed from central headquarters, it's slower for both bureaucratic and financial reasons, because all the money would come from one bank account. "So if somebody's spending money in Cleveland, that's your bank account at headquarters." And Cleveland could drain it, leaving nothing for Milwaukee and Phoenix. King explained that the franchise City Years could be controlled through a licensing agreement that was as stringent as Brown and Khazei wanted it to be. "That's why the YMCAs all look similar," Brown says, then laughs. "They probably send brand inspectors out."

But King also pointed out that the more complex the organization, the less likely it is to go the franchise route. Which is why, Brown says, department stores and law firms tend not to.

Of course, this much was theoretical. The real work of the consultant was to swoop down on City Year, talk to everyone, and figure out just what kind of a place it was, for that would dictate the way to grow. One key factor was the dynamic of the organization and whether it was into fast replication—or maintaining control. Another was the organization's complexity. The more complex, the stronger the argument for centralized control. City Year was pretty complex—not like a law firm, necessarily, but more than a donut shop. It also had certain philosophical standards to maintain—to train young people of all backgrounds, for example. "What if somebody didn't care about that?" Brown recalls being asked. It would be a problem, needless to say. Also, City Year was determined to address community needs *while* it trained a new generation of leaders, not do one or the other. And, finally, City Year had a national presence as it advocated in Washington and tried to instill a belief in the value of national service. In summary, King sized up Brown and Khazei as "very intense entrepreneurs," and he averred that they wouldn't be too happy to see someone in Omaha deciding what City Year was to be.

Powerful arguments all of them, but Brown and Khazei also knew that they could not afford to run a national organization, that they did want to expand rapidly to establish a national presence, and that they could build in the safeguards and controls that would allow them to make sure that any new City Years met their standards. To do that, King helped them develop what he terms "guideposts" to make sure that each new organization stuck with the program. The guideposts included minimum funding requirements, committed board members, fifty letters of support from community leaders including the mayor, and financial support from the school districts. On top of that, King helped develop managerial lines of responsibility back to the national office, even though managers' primary responsibility was still to their own operation.

By 2011, City Year gave birth to twenty-one City Years, starting in Columbia, South Carolina, as unlikely as that may sound. (Brown's parents took forty-two guesses to pick the state.) A City Year staffer had moved there and was begging to bring the operation along. And that's what it takes: one individual who is eager to do what the founders did and who will commit to doing it the way the founders did. Ultimately the organization was able to rapidly extend its reach nationally even as it stayed true to its organizational mandate. City Year found out what City Year was—and bottled it for wider distribution.

That said, growth is not easy, whichever way you go. It can be as hard to grow an organization as it was to start one in the first place. It is satisfying in that it demonstrates to the world that this idea of yours was just as necessary as you'd thought. But however many problems you had initially, you will have that many more when you expand. Which may be why most nonprofits don't grow at all. They create their operation, find their niche, and stay in it, content to do what they started out to do, and no more.

All of these approaches are fine, obviously. Go franchise, expand the central headquarters, stay as you are. You need to do only what you want to do. There is no requirement for you to be any other size than the one you are.

The Measure of Success

The successful growth of an organization—in fact, success in general—depends on being able to measure your outcomes, and an efficient system of measurement should be part of every strategic plan. Imagine driving a car that had none of the usual displays on the dashboard. No speedometer, fuel gauge, odometer, GPS. All you had were an ignition switch, steering wheel, accelerator, and brakes. A Model T, basically, only faster. You'd be able to keep this jalopy on the road, most likely, and moving. But you would have no idea how fast you were going, how far it was to your destination, how long it would take to get there, whether you had enough fuel to make the trip, or what sort of strain was being placed on the engine.

That's what it is like to manage a nonprofit organization that pays no attention to measurement. You can probably keep the organization going, but you won't know much else, such as whether you are doing anything useful or are operating efficiently.

To many people, measurements remind them of dry high school science experiments that involve beakers and conversion to the metric system. But they are much more like magic glasses that allow you to see things that are otherwise imperceptible but are vital to your well-being. Measurements indicate where you actually are, as opposed to where you wish you were. As the economist Michael Hammer once observed, "You cannot improve what you cannot measure." You recall that Geoffrey Canada had to completely redesign his school in Harlem when a close study of the school's operation revealed that it was achieving precious few of its stated goals. It would have been easier for everyone if that examination had never been undertaken, but it would have led only to a greater loss, and a hollow enterprise, one that was making stunning claims, but had no proof to back them up. That's the car that has no instrument panel, the driver bombing down the road with no idea where she is or where she is going, but happy to be on the move.

But it is not only your own position that you can determine with measurement. You can also see where you are compared with others. The fact is, nonprofits are in a competition no less than for-profits—not for profits but for market share, lower costs, and efficiency, among other measures, in their race to be the best in their field. For example, if you discover that it costs you twenty-seven cents to raise a dollar for your organization, but for your major competitor that figure is eighteen, you have a problem, and you should find out where those extra costs are coming from and how they can be cut. Your potential donors would be discouraged to learn of the higher cost, and irritated if you didn't address the issue. Not to mention that you'd be missing out on opportunities that the "extra" money could bring you.

Every area of the nonprofit's endeavor should be subject to this same kind of analysis. Compensation, costs of delivery, marketing—the list is virtually endless. But remember: just because you pay more for something doesn't necessarily mean that you are wasting money. It can certainly be worthwhile to pay 20 percent more than the industry average for a chief marketing officer if he is going to produce far better results. And, of course, some of those results are going to be intangible—improved morale or greater efficiency in the marketing effort. But the scrutiny alone can produce valuable insights about what you seek to accomplish and the manner in which you expect to accomplish it.

But that is all on the operations side—measuring the efficiency of the organization with an eye to squeezing out costs. A second set of measurements examines quality control and performance improvement. That is to say, are your clients happy with the services you are delivering? If you are providing psychological services, are clients waiting too long in the waiting room? Are your providers all first rate? Are billing procedures orderly and accurate? Is the facility pleasant and attractive? All these are measurable, and they are essential both for measuring current performance and for guiding improvement. They all assess the critical question that every nonprofit leader should be repeatedly asking herself: Am I doing a good job? How can I be sure? Is our work having an impact? How do I know? These questions are as pertinent to Darell Hammond with his playgrounds as they are to Jordan Kassalow and his eyeglasses. Is my product improving people's lives? If so, by how much? If by that much, how can I make it more?

Of course, the answers will depend on the questions. In the case of Kassalow, he might ask, How many eyeglasses have I been able to get on people's faces in the last twelve months? A useful data point, no doubt. But a more valuable one might be, How much of a difference did those glasses make to their wearers' lives? Could they then get a job? Were they able to read to their children? Some of the answers may go beyond the scope of the current work. It is not up to Kassalow to improve the employment outlook in rural India. But it is helpful to remember the idea that we have advanced before, when we discussed the differences between goals, mission, strategy, and actions. Kassalow's goal is not to be the biggest eyeglass distributor in the developing world. It is to improve vision to change lives. If lives are not improved, Kassalow has done nothing useful, no matter how many glasses he sells.

In nonprofits, as in other areas of the economy, there are two paths to greatness. The first is taken by the charismatic leader who, by force of his personality, is able to form an organization, inspire a following, and do impressive work. We admire such leaders, but we are dubious about them. Theirs is more the realm of religion than of doing good. For who is to say that such leaders are leading in a useful direction? Their say-so, no matter how eloquently expressed, is not sufficient.

Which brings us to the other path—that of collecting and taking advantage of information. We live in an information society. The amount you can pull up in a Google search is staggering, and there are many ways to drill down from there. The point is, even if you don't gather information relevant to your organization, somebody else has for theirs, and you don't want to be late to the party.

One caveat. We'd recommend that you *not* do your own research, but subcontract it out to an independent researcher, whose analysis will be more dispassionate and therefore more useful to you and to third parties you might want to share it with.

What, exactly, might you want to look into? One of the cross-field conceptual frameworks we believe in is the triad of *accessibility, acceptability,* and *outcome.* Accessibility is just what it sounds like: your program has to be reachable and usable by the population you are trying to serve. If a service can't easily be accessed, then it isn't much good, so effort should be exerted to lowering barriers. It should go without saying that a service for people with disabilities needs wheelchair ramps, or that one for a partly Latino clientele needs at least some bilingual providers. But you would be surprised at how many nonprofits overlook such obvious requirements. Acceptability is more individual. Kassalow might have offered contact lenses to the poorly sighted, except he was afraid that potential clients would find them difficult to use in parts of the world without clean water, and replacements would be hard to come by. The service needs to match the need. And, needless to say, outcomes are critical.

The quest for information should not be a sideline activity in your nonprofit. It needs to be ingrained, a pursuit that is shared by everyone in the organization. An inclination toward numbers, toward hard proof, rather than toward general impressions and wan hope. Hope, as they say, is not a strategy. But maintaining a numbers orientation is a huge undertaking, and even if you can weave this bias into your organization, you shouldn't expect a transformation in the first year. It will likely start to be noticeable in the second and not become entrenched until the third. It took a while, after all, for automobile designers to develop the elaborate dashboard display that we now take for granted. Right now, for many nonprofits, those dashboard readouts are there, but nonprofit managers haven't trained themselves to glance down. They should—in good times and bad. Nonprofits need to be built for the long haul, difficult as that can be. Good information is essential for nonprofits to flourish in the good times and more than hang on in the bad. Too often, information acquisition is the first thing to go when times turn tough. That is as foolish as for-profits abandoning R&D at the first sign of a downturn. Stick with it!

As Canada's example shows, the measurements aren't just for you. They are for others. It is one thing to tell people how well you are doing; it is another to back up your statements with objective evidence. Potential donors, be they individuals, foundations, corporations, or governments, want to see the real results, and who can blame them? Of course, precise measurement can also yield better financial results—and will redound doubly to your credit.

Forming Your Plan

In the search for meaning, it is always hard to decide which data to value, for so much depends on what you are trying to achieve—yet that decision, in turn, may depend on the data. And the very act of collecting information forces an evaluation of it. The results force hard choices, but in the evaluation of those results lies the purpose and thus the future of the organization.

With that in mind, make sure you have an appropriate system of measurements in place to be sure that the plan is delivering the desired outcomes as you move forward. Yes, you've researched this plan and thought it through in great detail, but no plan is foolproof, and if you don't measure as you go, you may find that the plan has taken you down the wrong path.

The time frame of a strategic plan is also important. It needs to be long enough to allow for a significant impact, but not so long that it seems endless. Our guess is that two or three years is becoming more prevalent than the Soviet-style Five-Year Plans. Two- to three-year plans should take about three to six months to put together, of which maybe half the time is spent with the board actively deliberating.

One tip: sometimes it is better not to call it a strategic plan, as such a formal term can seem too forbidding, as if the whole program were under review and jobs might be at stake. Better just to tell people, casually, that you are setting up a small short-term planning committee. Anything more, and employees sometimes get frightened.

Regardless of how it is framed, the strategic plan lays out the strategy for the organization to make good on its mission. From it flows everything—operating plan, personnel goals, budgetary requirements, fundraising targets. It lays out every aspect of the organization. Because that is the case, a financial assessment should be included, possibly with a feasibility study for a new fundraising campaign if it looks as though the new strategic plan is so ambitious that serious money will be needed. A strategic plan focused only on spending priorities is doomed to the dusty shelf.

Leading the Plan

As the founder, how should you act? At some level, this plan should be your initiative; otherwise, the organization won't seem to be seriously committed to it. But you should be careful not to make it seem as though it is *just* yours. Ideally, your leadership on this point, as on other major ones, should have a ghostly quality to it: your actions should seem to happen almost by themselves. In this we pay great heed to the Chinese philosopher Lao Tzu's advice: "A leader is best when people barely know he exists, when his work is done, his aim fulfilled, they will say, 'We did it ourselves.'" The wise leader leads the effort, but does not get out in front of it. He is not at the head of the parade, but has quietly formed it and ushered it along. With such initiatives, the sooner the whole organization takes possession of them, the better. As the founder, you should take pleasure that you and it act as one.

That said, the founder is only as good as the plan he enacts. Just as hardware requires software, and architects need blueprints, founders need plans to bring their organization into existence and into prosperity, and those founders are indispensable in making those plans happen. To a large extent, any plan is the social entrepreneur's vision, one that can be realized. Like the Constitution or any other founding document, it is a message that is clear and inspiring, and it will help create the little nation that is his social enterprise.

CHAPTER 16

The Money Side

Money Is Not a Dirty Word

WHEN YOU THINK OF REVENUE on a nonprofit ledger, you probably think of fundraising, and you are probably not thrilled at the prospect. Fundraising ranks with taxpaying as just about everyone's least favorite financial activity.

So—don't do it. Or don't if you can possibly avoid it. Fundraising should be your last resort when you need money, as you surely will. Nonprofit does not mean nonrevenue. You are fully entitled to make money, and lots of it. You just aren't allowed to keep it for yourself or distribute it to shareholders. It is only to be spent in pursuit of your mission, not on inflated salaries for your employees. (Indeed, the IRS has rules and regulations regarding fair salary determination.) So for revenue, made money works just as well as raised money.

Made money actually has lots of advantages over the raised kind. First, it is likely to be a much steadier source of revenue. Major gifts are capricious in the best of times, iffy in so-so ones, and likely to vanish altogether when times go bad. Plus, to many, earned income feels more respectable than the unearned variety, even though the latter might be harder won. Steady income can be a far more reliable indicator of market recognition than a cluster of gifts, as the money comes directly from a grateful user, not from a donor whose motivations can be hard to discern. What's more, if you are delivering a valued product or service, income is virtually limitless, whereas donations are likely to be capped by a finite donor base. Finally, let's face it: fundraising is a total drag—exhausting, dispiriting, draining—whereas straight-out money making can be something of a high.

If you're smart, you'll have been thinking of potential revenue streams from the get-go, and not turning your attention to them only after you've become the manager of a going concern. In fact, the chances are good that your beloved nonprofit would not be a going concern if you hadn't been thinking this way. The most obvious strategy for generating revenue is to charge something, heavily discounted, for the service you provide. If you are running a food program, you might charge a small sum for a meal—not enough to pay for it, but enough to recognize its value. Beyond that, take the revenue not as cash but as in-kind donations. For your food program, you could go around to caterers and restaurateurs to collect any food they have left over at the end of the night. Or wholesalers for that matter, on the same basis. Such food isn't money, but it might as well be, considering the benefits to the bottom line.

Not long ago, we received a proposal from a man trying to create a community of young people. We would not have been interested except for the beauty of its financing, which was based on a membership model. Every member had to pay a modest amount for the privilege of joining this community. The finances had been worked out such that the organization would be self-sufficient if it reached three thousand members. All too many of these start-ups want money right away, more money later, and more money after that. Well, this guy's approach was heaven: the philanthropic investor can get out with a clear conscience as soon as success emerges.

Jordan Kassalow: Putting the Profit in Nonprofit

Most of the social entrepreneurs we discuss in this book were fairly comfortable with the notion of riding on capitalistic incentives to deliver social benefits. It is why they were so successful. One is Jordan Kassalow. After he had that moment of revelation when he outfitted a nearly blind boy with glasses that brought him his first vision of the world, Kassalow spent another fifteen years working out the mechanics of getting more glasses on people's faces without his having to literally put them there. It took him that long to figure out the money. Would foundations pay for the glasses, he wondered, or would the individuals themselves? And if it were the individuals, how could Kassalow get the glasses to them? While he continued to work as an optometrist, he also studied the fundamentals of delivering product—how to source it, price it, and sell it—to the developing world. And, along with taking many trips to Latin America and India, he investigated international development and foreign policy so that he could operate more smoothly in poor countries where the need was most acute. Through it all, he continued to ponder the notion that he'd had from the very beginning, which was to use the basic precepts of capitalism to encourage local people in poor countries around the world to sell glasses to their neighbors. That proved to be the founding vision, as it were, of VisionSpring, which Kassalow created in 2002.

"To make a go of it, I knew I needed three things—a good idea, people, and money," he says. The idea was a go after his trips to Latin America. There, he examined about two thousand people with serious vision difficulties every week, of whom 70 percent needed glasses only; the remainder required medicine or surgery. Of that 70 percent, half could get by with glasses of the type people in the United States would find in a drugstore. That was his market, for those glasses could make the difference between self-sufficiency and dire poverty. As he says, "There was a huge economic drain throughout the developing world because of something that was so fixable with a product I could source in China for under a dollar."

That is when he had the final epiphany: to rely on capitalism to power this nonprofit. The profit motive would release a legion of eyeglasses salespeople, mostly women, throughout the developing world. They would bring with them what he terms a "business in a bag"—a store of eyeglasses to sell to people in need. When he tested the concept on eighteen saleswomen in India, a third broke even, a third lost money, and a third made money. It wasn't an overwhelmingly positive response, but it was enough. "It was enough to say, hey, we should keep giving it a go and find out, and that, very much the tenet of social enterprise, is to look for bright spots and start to understand why they work, and then ask a bunch more questions. And then eight things that you try don't work, but two will." That's how start-ups are. Most fail, and most of their ideas fail. So you need to grab on to the ones that succeed, because that is all you will ever have. Kassalow depended on the sales force. There simply weren't enough of what he called "philanthropical dollars" to accomplish the mission. "There are about a half billion people who need these glasses," he says. "Even if we raise tens of millions of dollars, we weren't going to make a dent in the problem." For that, he would need to harness the power of the market. "Then we can really scale it," he says.

Of course, once you enter the markets, you are participating in the market economy, and that means attending to issues that most social entrepreneurs ignore, such as price margins. Kassalow needed to make a profit, yes, but how much of one? Too much, and he would drive down sales. Too little, and he would not capture enough of the proceeds of any sale to reinvest in the organization. In the end, he settled on a fee that was pegged to 10 percent of the seller's monthly income.

What he calls the "supply chain logistics" were trouble, too. To assure himself of a steady supply of glasses, Kassalow needed to make use of the low-cost glasses made in China for Walmart, Kmart, Target, and other major stores. Now, how to get those glasses onto faces in such places as Bangladesh and rural Ghana? This is where capitalism helped, for Kassalow had by then started a for-profit glasses company in the United States, and he could make use of his knowledge of distribution systems. Distribution was no snap: from factory outlet to distribution point in Bangladesh, for example, it required fifty-seven different signatures, and it took six months to get it done. He was unable to reduce the number of signatures, but he did cut the process time in half to three months. But for the end sale, he realized he would need a network of salespeople in the field, whom he called "vision entrepreneurs." That developed slowly; the first eighteen vision entrepreneurs in India sold just eight hundred pairs of glasses in the first year. But soon Kassalow was adding dozens more vision entrepreneurs selling glasses on commission throughout the developing world. And the sales rose impressively, totaling close to one million pairs of glasses sold by the end of 2011.

But marketing problems remain. Oddly, despite the need, the hardest part of the process has been the end sale, chiefly because the potential customers do not always recognize the value of something they don't possess and may never have possessed, namely, eyesight. "Once they put on glasses, they have a seeing-is-believing moment, and they're immediate converts. But until then, people don't know what they're missing. They don't think there is anything broken that needs to be fixed."

It falls to the visionary, the salesperson, to create that awareness by getting glasses to the poorly sighted, one at a time. Lately, Kassalow has thought of getting the word out by putting the glasses attached to slender chains in public places, like pens in banks, for people to try—and including the now-readable contact information of a local vision entrepreneur for possible purchase.

Over time, Kassalow discovered that, much as he wanted the vision entrepreneurs to succeed, sale by sale they were proving to be too expensive for the organization to rely on them exclusively. They paid themselves by commission, yes, but they also required training and monitoring, which was pricey in these remote locations. Regretfully, Kassalow decided that he would need to supplement their efforts if he was to reach the penetration and scale he sought, and turned to other sales networks. That meant selling his glasses through existing health-related distribution systems, such as the world-class economic development organization called BRAC, which markets health products in Bangladesh. It is limited in that it is just one organization in one country, but it is a helpful model, in that, like a proper store, it is already geared up to warehouse, display, and sell medical products, including Kassalow's glasses.

Still, even this has involved some fine-tuning, now that Kassalow has learned that consumers are interested in prescription eyeglasses, not just the drugstore variety. To address this need, the resourceful Kassalow developed a hub-and-spoke strategy, in which he has created what amounts to a central depot, a "LensCrafters for the poor" as he calls it, that radiates out through spokes to the vision entrepreneurs that he likens to Avon ladies. The entrepreneurs sell the simple glasses out in the field, and relay more complicated requests to the hub, where an optometrist can handle them. The prescription glasses are particularly lucrative because they are sold at a higher profit margin. That means more money for the vision entrepreneur and, in turn, for VisionSpring.

Besides working out the revenue stream, Kassalow has performed a key assessment by tabulating the material benefit to the glasses wearer, too. Thanks to a three-year study by the University of Michigan School of Business, Kassalow can report that the glasses have increased wearers' productivity by 35 percent.[1] Not bad for a product he can source in China for seventy cents.

Using a For-Profit Model

For-profit companies create a market between buyers and sellers for the transfer of a good or service. Nonprofits try to do the same. But they are at a serious disadvantage because there is often too little money in the system to create the demand for what they offer. Programs for children, animals, or the indigent—few will pay for themselves. With most causes, the recipients who benefit are likely to be too diffuse or poor to be buyers. And some nonprofits prefer not to charge for their product, viewing it as a corruption to monetize an act of charity. It feels wrong to indulge in capitalism.

But at bottom, there isn't much difference between nonprofits and for-profits except the fundamental clientele. Sell eyeglasses on Fifth Avenue, and you're a for-profit. Sell them in sub-Saharan Africa, and you probably aren't. Not because there is anything wrong with for-profits, but simply because there isn't enough profit to be had in sub-Saharan Africa to lure a businessman interested in an attractive return on his investment. But, as Kassalow has demonstrated, that doesn't mean that the principles of capitalism can't be deployed to address some of the more intractable social issues of the nonprofit realm.

Corporate Revenue

If employing a capitalistic, market-based business model as a means of enhancing revenues doesn't fit with your organization, there are other options, even beyond the obvious one of straight-out fundraising. According to *Giving USA 2011,* corporate philanthropy technically makes up only 5 percent of all philanthropic donations,[2] but it is actually more than that if you include the promotional budgets of corporations. So you might think of looking at companies whose corporate missions parallel yours. And if a corporation can see a strategic payoff because of this alignment, it will view any funding not as a handout but as an investment. So it isn't begging to ask for it. It was under the promotional budget of Home Depot that Darell Hammond was able to receive the funding that got him going. But a lot of this type of contribution is made in kind. Musicians on Call, an organization we particularly like (and not just because Jeff's son, Michael Solomon, was its cofounder), received such a gift from Clear Channel, which owns eleven hundred radio stations across the country. Clear Channel selected Musicians on Call as its national charity for the first quarter of 2011, which amounted to about $20 million of free advertising. Of course, such a freebie doesn't come easily. Michael had recruited one of Clear Channel's senior executives for his board, and that executive had assiduously lobbied his own company for over five years before the benefit came through.

But that kind of money, or that kind of value, doesn't grow on trees. Rather it is the product of some strategic planning on the part of the nonprofit. First, as the Michael Solomon story suggests, you can't go in cold. You'll need to know someone. With Musicians on Call, the someone was perfect: highly connected to the organization and to the company being solicited. Note that even then it took five years to secure the gift. Beyond the connection, you should focus on the sense of alignment. Can you imagine that the company you're targeting really will get something of significant benefit out of any gift to you? If you can't see it, the company probably can't either. So move on to one that will.

Government Funding

The government at all levels—municipal, state, federal—is another source of funds. Acquiring those funds is generally a matter of grant writing but, with the government as in other arenas, it can help to know someone. And there are other types of government backing aside from a straight-out government grant. With the right information, you can present your organization as eligible for a money stream from an existing government program. If you are in the health field, for example, you might be eligible for Medicare or Medicaid benefits reimbursements from eligible patients. In any jurisdiction, if you want to improve your chances, you would do well to develop relationship with key officials. These kinds of opportunities make an argument for large boards, even for relatively small organizations; they extend the reach of your operation and expand your pool of contacts. Or, if an expanded board is too unwieldy, you can always divide the board in two—an advisory board that meets occasionally, and the formal governing body, more of an operational one, that meets more regularly. Most government grantmaking is sophisticated in that it demands carefully constructed proposals. Even when unsuccessful, using these applications as a learning and growing process is invaluable, especially if you seek and receive feedback on the failure.

By the same token, the staff are likely to be making contacts of their own in the course of routine business, and they should be trained to make full use of them, thinking strategically with the idea that this piece of business might lead to a more valuable one later on.

Good, Old-Fashioned Fundraising

It is almost inevitable that you will have to resort to fundraising. Virtually no one in the nonprofit world can escape it, no matter how high his or her position. In fact, the higher you are, the more likely you are to spend a significant portion of your time meeting with potential donors. The head of every organization from Harvard University to the local Little League dedicates a good portion of his job to raising money. And rest assured that no fundraiser ever bats a thousand. In fact, it's safe to say that if a professional baseball player struck out as often as typical fundraisers do, he'd be laughed out of the league. The failure rate is staggering. But take heart; your efforts are in service to a great cause. If you get turned down, the loss is theirs, not yours.

That said, all of our eighteen social leaders have had their share of disappointments, and all of them have responded with yet greater determination to press on, such is their commitment. Carolyn LeCroy of the Messages Project suffers from, shall we say, a mismatch between her resources and her aspirations. She would love to take her project to prisons in every state in the union, but the prisons themselves can't afford to support her efforts, and she finds it nearly impossible to raise significant revenue on her own with written appeals to local charities and potential donors. She can't afford to hire a marketing person to extend her reach, or a grant writer to solicit funds to float her. So she is left scrounging for small sums—a few hundred dollars in response to appeals to area churches, maybe fifty from the local Kiwanis Club after a speech there, and ten or twenty-five more kicked in by individual donors. "I am so grateful for all of it, believe me," she says. "Even five dollars makes a difference." She covers the balance by appealing to her most reliable source of funds: her Visa card. "But even that was maxed out at one point," she admits. Despite the adversity, she's going to find a way. "I'm not going to disappoint the mothers and fathers in prison who want to get a message out to their kids. I'm sorry, but I'm just not."

And even Kassalow, for all his determination to adopt for-profit business models for his glasses endeavor, has found that it is not enough. He'd hoped that the market would power the distribution of his glasses, but it hasn't yet. "These markets are deeply stalled," he admits. "It's going to take us a while to get them to work." In the meantime, he, too, has had to turn to "philanthropic capital," the seeking of which he admits is "one of the more challenging parts of an entrepreneur's job." He describes his own efforts as a combination of "hard grinding" and luck. A piece of the latter came when he happened to get himself invited to the home of George Soros, the billionaire investor. When all the guests were gathered, Soros went around to each one to ask who he was and what he did. This was before Kassalow had launched VisionSpring, but it was very much on his mind, and he told Soros about it, in a few well-chosen sentences. "He asked me a few questions and said it was a fascinating idea." Soros put Kassalow in touch with the director of his foundation—and told Kassalow to ask him for $50,000 to test the idea in India. The foundation people agreed to send him the money. That was the seed money to test out the first eighteen vision entrepreneurs, which launched the program.

Seeing how well the business idea went down with Soros, Kassalow entered some business plan competitions, winning the Yale–Goldman Sachs competition worth $25,000, and then copping a $120,000 grant from the World Bank's Development Marketplace Competition. The judges were taken by the explosive power of his seemingly simple idea. The success won him the attention of the Draper Richards Foundation in California, which applies a venture capital model to social enterprise. Taken by Kassalow, the foundation provided a $300,000 multiyear grant and took a seat on his board to provide steady mentoring. Then the Skoll Foundation, "the Academy Award of the social enterprise space," Kassalow says, gave him their Oscar, a three-year grant totaling nearly $1 million.

Large as these sums are, they have had to be in order for Kassalow to sustain his vision. Right now, only 41 percent of his budget is covered by sales. The rest is paid for by grants and private philanthropy. He is getting on track to alter this ratio and is optimistic that VisionSpring will cover its costs within the next five years.

The literature tells us that the greatest risk in nonprofit financing is to rely on foundation grants for operating support. Individual donors, government contracts, and third-party fees are all more reliable as ongoing revenue streams. Building as diversified a financial plan as possible is the wisest course of action.

CHAPTER 17

Making Your Exit

How Do You Know
When It Is Time to Go?

FEW FOUNDERS PLAN FOR THEIR EVENTUAL departure from their organization. They often put off the inevitability of leaving as if they would be able to stay there forever. In estate law, those who die intestate, without wills to account for their estates, create havoc as heirs scramble to determine who gets what. Founders who make no plans for their departure do something similar.

In fairness, the question of when to leave is virtually unique to nonprofits and their founders. There is no obvious equivalent on the for-profit side. For corporate chieftains, a looming sale or merger declares in bold letters that it is time for him to move to the exit lane. Cash out and go. On the nonprofit side, such exit signs are either nonexistent or invisible. Occasionally, a nonprofit will merge with another, possibly folding into it, giving you as the founder a good moment to take your leave. But otherwise the matter is rather subtle, like divining the moment when summer gives way to fall or when a long, entrenched recession finally ends. It takes that sort of sensitivity, to say nothing of humility, to realize that you have taken your idea as far as you can, and now, for the good of the organization, it's time to go. While for-profit businesses might be handed down through the generations, nonprofits belong to the community, not to the founder, and are far less likely to engage several generations of the founder's family.

As a general, very loose rule, the natural lifespan of the active job of the founder is probably somewhere in the eight- to fifteen-year range, but don't hold us to that. We know a woman who left before five, and it was the perfect time. We know others who are still going strong after thirty, and no one has any regrets. How do you know when you are overstaying your welcome? Basically, it's when the polarity on the magnet has been reversed. You are producing less than you consume, and because of that, your staff is too. The job doesn't generate energy or ideas or enthusiasm, but somehow drains them, and the problems outnumber the solutions.

At the time of this writing, only one of our sample of eighteen social entrepreneurs has actually left his organization, although several of the other veterans have given it serious thought. It is a sign of their ability as managers, though, that they could say exactly why they are staying on and when they will know it is time to go.

City Year's Michael Brown has been at his post for over twenty years. Why does he stay? "The way I look at it is, you have to recognize that there are phases to this work, and basically, you have to sign up for each phase. And you have to be all in. Each phase, I start with a self-assessment. Am I excited about that phase? Is it still fresh? Do I still have something to offer? Or should somebody else step in? And would others, like the board, agree with that? There needs to be some external check on all of that. I don't have enough self-knowledge."

Brown performed this assessment not long before we conducted the interview for this book, and, as he says, he "re-signed up" with enthusiasm, thrilled with the potential of the organization he has helped build. "I've never been more excited about being here, never been more excited about the work, never, ever felt this way about the organization's potential," he declares. He believes that the organization is now finally on the verge of establishing the measurements that will provide convincing proof of the value of national service. And he is thrilled with the management team he has assembled. But there is more than that. He notes that President Kennedy used to define happiness as engagement, and engagement as happiness. "Happiness to him was using his powers to the fullest along lines of excellence," says Brown. He feels fully utilized at City Year and believes that it has brought out the best he has to offer, resources that he doesn't think could be deployed so effectively, and happily, in another setting.

There will inevitably come a time, though, when your engagement will loosen somewhat, and the feeling of happiness dip. Pay attention. Is this temporary, or has it been progressing for a while? In this critical interplay between head and heart, you'll discover that both are committed, or neither are. If interest abates, start to think about what will restore your vitality. Life is brief, so you owe it to yourself and to others to put your energy where it can do the most good.

Founder's Syndrome

As a founder, you need to realize that there is a difference between your organization and your life. That is to say, your baby is not a baby, and it is not yours. This brings us back to the fundamental truth about nonprofits, the one that makes them so distinctive. To the extent that they are owned at all, they are owned by the community. Not by you. Again, you are merely the steward, and a temporary one at that. Like building anything, starting a nonprofit requires a healthy ego. But it will require an even healthier one to let it go, confident that your ego will survive intact.

217

Some people forget that. A founder may identify so much with her organization that she cannot accept that she is not the only person who could possibly lead it. Many flatterers have told her so, after all, and history confirms it. But organizations can change over time, and so can founders. Both can shift in style and approach as they age, adding other new interests, connections, and resources that may become less compatible. Where there was once a total identification of leader and led, there may begin a parting that can ultimately lead to a breach. There is a difference, after all, between then and now, and often it is a profound one. And it can happen that founders stop being right for their own organizations—and be the last to know it.

This scenario is not universal by any means, but it is common enough to have acquired a name: Founder's Syndrome. It's not a medical malady, but it is pernicious all the same. For founders have been known to damage their organizations and their own reputations in their determination to hang on to power too long.

"I only want to be called founder," jokes Darell Hammond when asked about the syndrome. "And I want my SUV waiting for me, air-conditioned to sixty-two degrees." Then he turns serious. "No, I've been cautious about the fact that cult of personality's not going to grow this thing. Sure, I'm the founder, and that carries a significant amount of influence and weight. But I try to be open, so that whether I am right or wrong, I support the decision we reach as an organization." To the extent that Founder's Syndrome invests the founder with godlike powers, humility is the perfect antidote.

All the other founders in our group of eighteen would say something similar. But we do know of others, outside the eighteen, who have succumbed, and it can lead to a clash between the founder and the board she is supposed to serve. When a founder becomes imperious, the board is about the only entity that is able to restore order. For any organization, a profound conflict between the board and the leader is disastrous, for it leaves the board no way to rise above the fray. Ideally, above the fray is where the board is always positioned, and thus able to view the operation of the organization, and the work of its leader, with considerable dispassion. It should work as the regulator that promotes the smooth running of a nonprofit, keeping every element, including the leader, in balance within the whole.

Happily, few disputes ever reach an impasse that results in the founder's being ousted. It is the rare founder who will risk the stigma of being bounced from her own organization. But power can be seductive, and some founders fail to see that they are wielding it unwisely and that their management decisions are benefiting only themselves. When the temptation to thrive on power arises, it is time to go. Past time, actually. Best practices tell us that the board should annually evaluate the CEO. This is often ignored, most especially with a CEO-founder who selected most of the board members. Yet if this evaluation is done well and with integrity, it is an important component of long-term executive sustainability.

The Succession Plan

The most effective organizations develop a succession plan long before one might be needed. Jay Feinberg, of the Gift of Life, has been working on one for a while. "If I get run over by a truck tomorrow, God forbid, then what happens?" he asks. "That thought weighs heavily on my mind." He takes some comfort in the fact that, as he says, the Gift of Life will continue, by virtue of the fact that it is a functioning business as a tissue bank. "We've got the right people in place and the right redundancies in place to keep our tissue bank going for many years to come, with or without me." However, the fundraising aspect of his job is not nearly so secure, as right now, Feinberg himself is the main, if not only, draw. That part is worrisome, he admits. But he is working on it.

It is never easy to leave, and not only because this leave taking can evoke feelings of great loss. More, it's because you're leaving your home, this enthralling community you've built. One that has a religious aspect, even, as it strains for a higher purpose and, for all the many difficulties, is living the dream you inspired. You will have given a lot to create this vision, and it is to your credit that there will be a lot to miss when you are gone.

Eventually that day will come. It won't mean a total break, or at least it shouldn't. You can stay on in some more limited capacity, either as chairman of the board or in some emeritus function that is comfortable for you and the organization. But the transition will mark a change for you, and it is one that you'll need to prepare for, both emotionally and practically. Darell Hammond has been thinking about the timing. KaBOOM! marked its fifteenth anniversary in 2011, and, at the time of this writing, a documentary on the organization is being developed. "So I'm committed here at least until then. And I will probably need some decompression time after that," he says. Echoing Michael Brown, Hammond calls himself "an all-in or all-out guy." He is not anywhere close to out yet. "I certainly haven't been able to think about anything else, and haven't had any reason to." He gets regular offers, but they only remind him how much he prefers to stay in his current post.

When your time does come to step away from day-to-day operations, be mindful. Orchestrate your departure with care, far more care than you gave to your arrival, which was probably haphazard. Work out any new arrangement with your current nonprofit well in advance and in some detail, so that everyone knows what to expect and you can be sure the transition feels right.

Try to imagine what it will feel like to no longer be the star of your own show. It might help to take a lengthy vacation or a serious trip to mark the break, so that you can return to your new life in a completely new frame of mind. Have another piece of work lined up. Take the skills that you have developed and bring them to a new, possibly larger arena. Your nonprofit was probably local, but you're ready for something more—larger audiences, bigger impact, greater scope. You have built a nonprofit, but it has also built you, and you can use your new skills, new arts, to do even greater good.

EPILOGUE

The Value of
Leadership

ONE ASPECT OF THE EXTRAORDINARY EIGHTEEN members of our sample has been so obvious that we have not even thought to mention it: their leadership skills. They are so abundant, so winning, and so widely on display that we have tended to view them as standard-issue stuff, and no more worthy of comment than their face having two eyes, a nose, and a mouth with teeth in it.

But as we think over what these social leaders have done, and how they have done it, we return to their leadership skills over and over. After all, this is not a time that is particularly open to leadership, much as people claim to crave it. Too many have given in to the skepticism of our day. Squeezed financially, pressed for time, most people's lives are so crammed, their spirits so depleted, they may have persuaded themselves that they have no time, space, or energy for idealism of the sort that our social entrepreneurs are promoting. And given that so many of our political leaders have disappointed us, it is a great accomplishment of these social entrepreneurs to persuade anyone to warm to the notion of leadership again. It takes a strong leader with a big heart to do all this.

A good leader is larger than life, and makes life bigger for her presence. She draws people to her and makes them feel better for being close. For these eighteen leaders, that magnetism is manifest in a variety of ways, be it the can-do dynamism of Anne Heyman, the social vision of Darell Hammond, the inspiring personal history of Jay Feinberg, or the artistic commitment of Sara Green, to name just a few. All eighteen have their areas of interest in the world, and all are compelling.

Daring to say the least, none of the eighteen have backed away from any major challenge, or so it would seem, no matter how daunting. Instead, they seem to relish it, eager—almost as if they were spectators, not participants—to see how they will handle this one. Starting a nonprofit and keeping it going—few things in public life are harder, but it is characteristic of these eighteen that "hard" is not a concept they've given much thought to. Any difficulties are just problems that haven't yet been solved—but soon will be. Because failure is not an option, they have nothing to fear.

As representatives of an older generation, we have likewise been impressed by how comfortable the eighteen have been with current technology, from Facebook to Twitter, and how much they've relied on it to boost the impact of their resources. New technology is a hallmark of the rising generation of social visionaries, and we expect that social networks and their successor technologies will radically transform philanthropy for the better. The social leaders profiled in this book have mastered these technologies and are using them to extend their scope.

As with political messages and commercial products, the ideas of our eighteen are fairly simple, but their impact has been profound. Kassalow's glasses, bringing life into focus, are possibly the best example, but all of them have a kind of built-in multiplier effect, making much out of much less. Rebecca Onie's prescription pad redefined medicine. Mark Hanis's campaign has allowed individuals to help end genocide. All of these ideas run deep, and testify to the audacity of these eighteen leaders.

And all eighteen are extremely focused. None of them have allowed themselves to be distracted from their main objective; rather, they will do whatever is needed to advance the cause. Yet despite their many sacrifices, none of them are Gradgrinds, turned surly and unpleasant by overwork. No—perhaps fueled by an essential optimism, they are able to retain their good cheer in the face of daunting challenges, confident that such challenges will lead to better days ahead. They are compelling, often hilarious speakers, full of insight and stories. And they are open to all comers, reflective of the pluralistic society in which they operate. After all, philanthropy is the love of all mankind, and it engages every corner of society, rich and poor, all ethnicities and genders, and these social entrepreneurs are comfortable in the entire realm.

But the most impressive quality of the eighteen may be that they will not be denied. No is just a prelude to yes, and they have no doubt that yes will come. If not tomorrow, then the next day or the day after that. Such optimism can seem delusional to those who aren't used to it. But these eighteen make it enticing, if not addictive. At heart, all eighteen preach the same message—the message of yes. In a world of no, they speak only of the yes: of solutions, of belief, of opportunity, of hope, of affirmation, of uplift, of possibility. Yes has to be one of the more seductive words in the language. Marriages all begin with it. It's the message of politicians and ministers. Yes is the theme of the eighteen, too. Each of them brings a different intonation, but all have a common meaning. It's yes for a better life tomorrow. And if you are to follow their example, yes should be your word, too. To hear and to say. Say it as they do—forcefully, gladly, convincingly, and often. Yes!

PART FOUR

Resources

"*Please*, sir — ten bucks more and
I can sign up for a fund-raising
course at the university!"

RESOURCE A

Index of
Nonprofit Resources

A RANGE OF INFORMATION ON NONPROFITS is presented in this resource under the following topics:

- Who helps philanthropy as a whole
- Who helps social entrepreneurs
- Who helps nonprofits be more effective
- Who helps staff do their jobs
- Who helps boards govern
- Who helps in next-generation funding
- Who writes about philanthropy and the nonprofit sector— periodicals
- Who teaches about the nonprofit sector—academic programs

Who Helps Philanthropy as a Whole

BBB Wise Giving Alliance (www.bbb.org/us). The alliance provides reporting and advisory services pertaining to national and

We gratefully acknowledge the assistance of the Council on Foundations; much of the information contained here comes directly from its Web site, www.cof.org. For foundations, membership in the Council on Foundations and other infrastructure organizations represents a strategic combination of good philanthropic citizenship and excellent member services.

international fundraising, as well as for nonprofit organizations that solicit contributions from the public. Its purpose is to maintain sound standards in the field of philanthropy and to aid wise giving through advisory reports to contributors. The alliance is a merger of the National Charities Information Bureau and the Council of Better Business Bureaus Foundation and its Philanthropic Advisory Service.

Charity Navigator (www.charitynavigator.org). This is the nation's largest and most-used evaluator of charities. In an effort to help donors make informed decisions, its professional analysts have developed an unbiased, objective, numbers-based rating system to assess the financial health of over five thousand of America's best-known charities. Charity Navigator creates evaluations that are easy to understand and available to the public free of charge in an effort to advance a more efficient and responsive philanthropic marketplace.

The Foundation Center (www.foundationcenter.org). Established in 1956, the Foundation Center is a leading source of information about philanthropy worldwide. Through data, analysis, and training, it connects people who want to change the world to the resources they need to succeed. The Center maintains the most comprehensive database on U.S. and, increasingly, global grantmakers and their grants—a robust, accessible knowledge bank for the sector. It also operates research, education, and training programs designed to advance knowledge of philanthropy at every level.

Giving Institute (www.aafrc.org). The Giving Institute publishes *Giving USA,* the annual yearbook on American philanthropy, and supports research and education. It continues to provide financial support, expertise, and leadership to the foundation world and works in partnership with it to advance philanthropy and promote ethics in the fundraising profession.

GuideStar (www.guidestar.org). The mission of GuideStar is to revolutionize philanthropy by providing information that advances transparency, enables users to make better decisions, and encourages charitable giving. To that end, GuideStar has created and is constantly updating a database of information on all IRS-recognized 501(c) nonprofit organizations eligible to receive tax-deductible contributions.

Independent Sector (www.independentsector.org). Independent Sector is the leadership forum for charities, foundations, and corporate giving programs committed to advancing the common good in America and around the world. This nonpartisan coalition of approximately 550 organizations leads, strengthens, and mobilizes the charitable community in order to fulfill the vision of a just and inclusive society and a healthy democracy of active citizens, effective institutions, and vibrant communities. Since its founding in 1980, Independent Sector has sponsored groundbreaking research, fought for public policies that support a dynamic nonprofit sector, and created unparalleled resources so that staff, boards, and volunteers can improve their organizations and better serve their communities.

Indiana University Center on Philanthropy (www.philanthropy.iupui.edu). This leading academic center is dedicated to increasing the understanding of philanthropy and improving its practice through research, teaching, and public service. Its cutting-edge programs and initiatives provide nonprofits, donors, and scholars with the resources they need to make a difference.

National Committee for Responsive Philanthropy (www.ncrp.org). The National Committee for Responsive Philanthropy

(NCRP) works with leaders in the philanthropic community and the recipients of giving to increase public accountability by philanthropies. It conducts research, compiles statistics, and publicizes reports in the philanthropic field.

Who Helps Social Entrepreneurs

Acumen Fund (www.acumenfund.org). Acumen Fund's purpose is to help end poverty by changing how the world addresses it. Acumen Fund champions the use of patient capital, understood as a debt or equity investment in an early-stage enterprise providing low-income consumers with access to health care, water, housing, alternative energy, or agricultural inputs. Investing patient capital allows for strengthening and scaling of business models that effectively serve the poor.

Ashoka (www.ashoka.org). Ashoka is a global association of leading social entrepreneurs, providing living stipends, professional support, and access to a global network of peers in seventy countries. In coordination with the global community, Ashoka develops models for collaboration and designs infrastructure needed to advance the field of social entrepreneurship and the citizen sector.

> **Youth Venture** (www.genv.net). Youth venture was begun in 1996 by Ashoka to inspire and invest in teams of young people to design and launch their own lasting social ventures, enabling them to have the transformative experience of leading positive social change. These Youth Venturers start businesses, civil society organizations, and informal programs that address all kinds of social issues, including poverty, health, the elderly, the environment, education, diversity issues, and the arts. Youth Venture helps them through the process of designing and launching their ventures, providing guidance and how-tos.

Change.org (www.change.org). Change.org is an organizing platform enabling anyone, anywhere to start his or her own grassroots campaign. The mission is to build an international network of people empowered to fight for what's right locally, nationally, and globally.

Echoing Green (www.echoinggreen.org). Echoing Green invests in and supports emerging social entrepreneurs in launching new organizations that deliver bold, high-impact solutions. Through a two-year fellowship program, it helps its network develop new solutions to society's most difficult problems. Its social entrepreneurs and their organizations work to solve deeply rooted social, environmental, economic, and political inequities to ensure equal access and to help all individuals reach their potential.

GlobalGiving.org (www.globalgiving.org). GlobalGiving connects donors with grassroots projects around the world. The site creates an efficient, open, thriving marketplace that connects people who have community- and world-changing ideas with people who can support them.

Harvard Business School Social Enterprise Initiative (www.hbs .edu/socialenterprise). The Social Enterprise Initiative aims to generate knowledge and to inspire, educate, and support current and emerging leaders in all sectors in applying management skills to create social value. The Social Enterprise Initiative engages with leaders in the nonprofit, for-profit, and public sectors to generate and disseminate practicable resources, tools, and knowledge with the ultimate goal of bettering society.

Net Impact (www.netimpact.org). Net Impact is an international nonprofit organization with a mission to inspire, educate, and equip individuals to use the power of business to create a more socially and environmentally sustainable world. Spanning six continents, its membership makes up one of the most influential networks of professionals and students in existence today. Net Impact members are current and emerging leaders in corporate social responsibility, social entrepreneurship, nonprofit management, international development, and environmental sustainability who are actively improving the world.

New Profit (www.newprofit.com). New Profit is a national venture philanthropy fund that seeks to harness America's spirit of innovation and entrepreneurship to help solve our country's biggest social problems. The fund's major focus is the social mobility of low-income Americans, pursued through a range of strategies designed to help build an environment in which all social entrepreneur-led organizations may realize their full potential for social impact.

Nonprofit Finance Fund (www.nonprofitfinancefund.org). Nonprofit Finance Fund is one of the nation's leading community development financial institutions, focusing exclusively on nonprofits. Services include financing, consulting, and advocacy. Multiple offices are spread across the United States.

Omidyar Network (www.omidyar.com). Omidyar Network is a philanthropic investment firm dedicated to harnessing the power of markets to create opportunity for people to improve their lives. eBay founder Pierre Omidyar and wife, Pam, established the Omidyar Network based on the principles of access, connection, and ownership to invest in and help scale innovative organizations to catalyze economic, social, and political change. The Omidyar Network makes investments in for-profit companies as well as grants to nonprofit organizations, with social impact being the unifying criterion for investment.

Catherine B. Reynolds Foundation Program in Social Entrepreneurship at NYU's Robert F. Wagner Graduate School of Public Service (www.nyu.edu/reynolds). The Catherine B. Reynolds Foundation Program in Social Entrepreneurship supports and trains a new generation of leaders in public service. The program includes undergraduate and graduate students committed to realizing pattern-breaking solutions to society's most intractable problems. The program also integrates the field of social entrepreneurship into the greater NYU community.

Schwab Foundation for Social Entrepreneurship (www .schwabfound.org). The Schwab Foundation for Social Entrepreneurship, in partnership with the World Economic Forum, provides platforms at the regional and global levels to highlight and advance leading models of sustainable social innovation.

Skoll Centre for Social Entrepreneurship at Oxford University (www.sbs.ox.ac.uk/centres/skoll/Pages/default.aspx). The Skoll Centre is a leading academic entity for the advancement of social entrepreneurship worldwide, fostering innovative social transformation through education, research, and collaboration. This is accomplished by developing talent, advancing research, and creating a collaborative hub for the dissemination of information to this emerging field.

> **Social Edge** (www.socialedge.org). Social Edge is a program of the Skoll Foundation that was inspired by Jeff Skoll's commitment to connecting people with shared passions. Social Edge is the global online community where social entrepreneurs and other practitioners of the social benefit sector connect to network, learn, inspire, and share resources.

Social Enterprise Alliance (www.se-alliance.org). The Social Enterprise Alliance (SEA) is the leading membership organization in North America for social enterprises, service providers, nonprofit organizations, corporations, and venture capitalists; it is actively building the field of social enterprise through networking opportunities, educational forums, strategic partnerships, and impact legislation. With nearly seven hundred members, SEA connects the growing community of social enterprise by hosting learning and networking opportunities throughout the United States and Canada.

Social Innovation Exchange (www.socialinnovationexchange .org). Social Innovation Exchange (known as SIX) is a global community of individuals and organizations committed to promoting social innovation and growing the capacity of the field. Their aim is to improve the methods with which our societies find better solutions to such challenges as aging, climate change, inequality, and health care.

Social Venture Network (www.svn.org). Social Venture Network (SVN) connects, supports, and inspires business leaders and social entrepreneurs in expanding practices that build a just and sustainable economy. SVN does this through relationship building, incubating emerging organizations, and fostering collaboration.

Who Helps Nonprofits Be More Effective

Aspen Institute—Program on Philanthropy and Social Innovation (www.aspeninstitute.org/psi). This program seeks to inform and maximize the impact of grantmaking foundations, nonprofit organizations, social enterprises, and public-private partnerships through leadership development initiatives, convenings, and communications so that each can contribute to the good of society at home and abroad. The program's theory of change rests on the premise that if leaders have clarity about their values, are collaborative in their approach to problem solving, and are aware of the strategies and potential partnerships available to them, they are more likely to succeed in advancing the social good. The program also hosts the Aspen Philanthropy Group, an agenda-setting body of foundation, nonprofit, and private-sector leaders at the cutting edge of change. The issues its members identify are subsequently considered in cross-sector working groups, with the aim of gaining consensus where possible and spurring collaborative action.

Association for Research on Nonprofit Organizations and Voluntary Action (www.arnova.org). The Association for Research on Nonprofit Organizations and Voluntary Action (ARNOVA) is an open forum that brings together researchers, scholars, and practitioners from around the world and works to strengthen the research community in the emerging field of nonprofit and philanthropic studies. ARNOVA brings together both theoretical and applied interests, helping scholars gain insight into the day-to-day concerns of third-sector organizations, while providing nonprofit professionals with research they can use to improve the quality of life for citizens and communities. Principal activities include an annual conference, publications, electronic discussions, and special interest groups.

CharityChannel (www.charitychannel.com). CharityChannel is the first and largest online professional network created by and for colleagues who serve exempt organizations. The CharityChannel community is made up of nonprofit-sector professionals from around the world who volunteer their time, advice, information, tips, and articles for the benefit of the nonprofit community.

Idealist (www.idealist.org). Idealist connects people, organizations, and resources to help build a world where all people can live free and dignified lives. It has a searchable network of more than thirty thousand nonprofit and community organizations in 165 countries, which can be browsed by name, location, or mission; a searchable list of volunteer opportunities and job openings; and extensive listings of events, programs, and publications. News articles, commentaries, reports, and essays related to NGOs are updated frequently.

National Center for Charitable Statistics (http://nccs.urban.org). The National Center for Charitable Statistics (NCCS) is the national repository of data on the nonprofit sector in the United States. Its mission is to develop and disseminate high-quality data on nonprofit organizations and their activities for use in research on the relationships between the nonprofit sector, government, the commercial sector, and the broader civil society. Working closely with the IRS and other government agencies, private-sector service organizations, and the scholarly community, NCCS builds compatible national, state, and regional databases and develops uniform standards for reporting on the activities of charitable organizations.

National Center on Nonprofit Enterprise (www.nationalcne .org/). The National Center on Nonprofit Enterprise (NCNE) helps nonprofit organizations make wise economic decisions to efficiently and effectively pursue their social missions. NCNE's extensive network of academic researchers, business leaders, and nonprofit practitioners form the backbone of NCNE's comprehensive program of educational activities and services that address the critical economic and decision-making issues facing the nonprofit sector.

National Council of Nonprofits (www.councilofnonprofits.org). The National Council of Nonprofits works through its member state associations to amplify the voices of America's local community-based nonprofit organizations, help them engage in critical policy issues affecting the sector, manage and lead more effectively, collaborate and exchange solutions, and achieve greater impact in their communities. The Resources section of the National Council of Nonprofits' Web site features an extensive collection of information, articles, tools, and various other resources of interest to nonprofit leaders.

Network for Good (www.networkforgood.org). One of the leading online charitable-giving resources, Network for Good helps nonprofits raise money on their own Web sites and on social networks with free and low-cost fundraising tools. The Network for Good Online Learning Center offers a wealth of resources and training to help with such tasks as online fundraising, donor engagement, and Web site development.

Society for Nonprofit Organizations (www.snpo.org). The Society for Nonprofit Organizations is a nonprofit organization that provides nonprofit staff members, volunteers, and board members with resources and information to work more effectively and efficiently toward accomplishing their mission.

TechSoup (www.techsoup.org). TechSoup is a nonprofit organization that provides other nonprofits and libraries with technology that empowers them to fulfill their missions and serve their communities. As part of that goal, TechSoup provides technology products and information geared specifically to the unique challenges faced by nonprofits and libraries. Learning resources, including articles, blogs, free webinars, and forums led by expert hosts are available to all users.

Who Helps Staff Do Their Jobs

Association of Fundraising Professionals (www.afpnet.org). The Association of Fundraising Professionals represents more than twenty-seven thousand members in 180 chapters throughout the United States, Canada, Mexico, and China working to advance philanthropy through advocacy, research, education, and certification programs. It is committed to preparing its members, the profession, and the sector to respond to the challenges of a dynamic philanthropic environment.

Association of Professional Researchers for Advancement (www.aprahome.org). The Association of Professional Researchers for Advancement (APRA) is an international organization for fundraisers who specialize in fundraising research, analytics, and relationship management. APRA is committed to providing leading-edge educational and networking opportunities to its members and the greater fundraising community, establishing and promoting high professional standards and ethical guidelines, and providing advocacy and a representative voice for the profession. Through educational and networking opportunities, publications, and community involvement, APRA offers opportunities and services that enable members to effectively meet the needs of their organizations while maintaining the highest ethical standards in an increasingly dynamic technological environment.

The Communications Network (www.comnetwork.org). The network promotes communications as an essential and integral component of grantmaking. In support of that mission, it provides leadership on the strategic role of communications in philanthropy, expands and enhances the communications capacity of grantmakers, and offers grantmakers the services and resources to communicate more effectively both internally and externally.

Foundation Financial Officer's Group (www.ffog.org). The Foundation Financial Officer's Group is a nonprofit membership organization of financial and investment officers of large, private foundations in the United States and abroad (defined as those with at least $200 million in assets).

Grant Professionals Association (www.grantprofessionals.org). The Grant Professionals Association (GPA; formerly known as the American Association of Grant Professionals) is a nonprofit membership association that supports an international community of grant professionals committed to serving the greater public good by practicing the highest ethical and professional standards. GPA serves as a leading authority and resource for the practice of grantsmanship in all sectors of the field and promotes positive relationships between grant professionals and their stakeholders. Through an array of professional growth and development services, GPA enhances the public image and recognition of the profession within the greater philanthropic, public, and private funding communities.

Grants Managers Network (www.gmnetwork.org). The Grants Managers Network (GMN) improves grantmaking by advancing the knowledge, skills, and abilities of grants management professionals and by leading grantmakers to adopt and incorporate effective practices that benefit the philanthropic community. GMN provides a forum for the exchange of information about grants management and its relevance to efficient and effective grantmaking. GMN offers training and tools that members need to succeed in their jobs and advance to leadership positions in the field.

Technology Affinity Group (www.tagtech.org). The Technology Affinity Group is a technology forum for professionals working in philanthropy. It seeks to advance best practices in technology through a network of technical and nontechnical foundation staff.

Who Helps Boards Govern

boardnetUSA (www.boardnetusa.org). boardnetUSA is a unique Web site dedicated to the express purpose of connecting nonprofit boards and new leaders. The site is designed to be a common technological platform for a national collaborative network of communities working locally to enhance nonprofit board governance. This growing network of community partners works together on common themes, such as populating boardrooms, as well as individually developing services tailored to their local markets.

BoardSource (www.boardsource.org). BoardSource is dedicated to advancing the public good by building exceptional nonprofit boards and inspiring board service. BoardSource is the premier source of cutting-edge thinking and resources related to nonprofit boards; it strives to support and promote excellence in board service and engages and develops the next generation of board leaders. BoardSource provides knowledge and resources for nonprofit leaders through workshops, training, assessment tools, an extensive Web site, and a membership program.

Who Helps in Next-Generation Funding

21/64 (www.2164.net). 21/64 is a nonprofit consulting division of the Andrea and Charles Bronfman Philanthropies specializing in intergenerational philanthropy, values clarification, and strategic grantmaking. It uses a multigenerational approach to understanding generational personalities, motivational values, and visions to help families define and achieve their individual and collective goals across generations.

Emerging Practitioners in Philanthropy (www.epip.org). Emerging Practitioners in Philanthropy (EPIP) is a network of professionals at foundations, government and corporate grantmaking entities, and philanthropy support organizations who seek to confront generational issues in the grantmaking community. EPIP works toward its mission through networking opportunities for its constituents, leadership development programs, and advocacy efforts to enhance the presence of the new generations of leaders in the philanthropic sector.

Resource Generation (www.resourcegeneration.org). Resource Generation offers a variety of programs for young people with wealth to explore how their financial resources relate to social justice and provides tools for them to take action. It offers forums to promote cross-class and intergenerational dialogues about money, class, and philanthropy.

YES! (www.yesworld.org). YES! is a nonprofit organization that connects, inspires, and collaborates with young changemakers in building thriving, just, and sustainable ways of life for all. YES! works at the meeting point of internal, interpersonal, and systemic transformation. Its popular Jam conference series provides a safe and transformative context within which to honestly explore issues of significance to privileged young people committed to social change.

YouthGive (www.youthgive.org). YouthGive helps grow the next generation of compassionate givers and global citizens, believing that everyone can be a philanthropist. YouthGive engages children and youth in philanthropy as a critical component to instilling lifelong habits of compassion, generosity, and civic engagement.

Youth Leadership Institute (www.yli.org). The Youth Leadership Institute builds communities where young people and their adult allies come together to create positive social change. It designs and implements community-based programs that provide youth with leadership skills in the areas of drug and alcohol abuse prevention, philanthropy, and civic engagement. Building on these real-world program experiences, it creates curricula and training programs that foster social change efforts across the nation, all while promoting best practices in the field of youth development.

Who Writes About Philanthropy and the Nonprofit Sector—Periodicals

Advancing Philanthropy (www.afpnet.org/publications /advancing_philanthropy). Published bimonthly by the Association of Fundraising Professionals, *Advancing Philanthropy* is an idea and strategy magazine for fundraisers in all sectors. With detailed reports and analyses of current trends, it educates, informs, and challenges the development community, giving readers practical applications and how-to articles, new research, interviews with donors, and tips and ideas from peers in the fundraising profession.

Alliance Magazine (www.alliancemagazine.org). A monthly magazine providing news and analysis of what's happening in the philanthropy and social investment sectors across the world. It also acts as a forum for exchange of ideas and experiences among practitioners. In addition to news and conference reports, articles, book reviews, and opinion columns, each issue has a special in-depth feature on a key aspect of philanthropy and social investment, with contributors from around the world and expert guest editors.

Associations Now (www.asaecenter.org/publicationsresources/). A monthly magazine for association executives published by the American Society of Association Executives and the Center for

Association Leadership. It delivers essential information and ideas that empower associations to master challenges, invoke imagination, and act decisively to create a better world. The January issue each year is devoted to addressing the needs of boards and other volunteer leaders.

BBB Wise Giving Guide (www.bbb.org/charity). A semiannual magazine published by the BBB Wise Giving Alliance. It includes a summary of the latest results of the alliance's national charity evaluations, along with a cover story about giving tips or charity accountability issues.

Blue Avocado (www.blueavocado.org). *Blue Avocado* is a nonprofit online magazine for community nonprofits. Published monthly as an e-newsletter, *Blue Avocado* aspires to high-quality journalism that speaks for and from the people in community-based nonprofits. It also features the popular Board Café column—a stand-alone publication until 2008—which offers a menu of ideas, information, opinions, news, and resources to help board members give and get the most out of board service.

Chronicle of Philanthropy (www.philanthropy.com). The newspaper of the nonprofit world, *Chronicle of Philanthropy* features news and information for charity leaders, fundraisers, grantmakers, and others involved in the philanthropic enterprise. Along with news, it offers such service features as lists of grants, fundraising ideas and techniques, statistics, reports on tax and court rulings, summaries of books, and a calendar of events. A subscription to the biweekly publication includes full access to the Web site database and email news updates.

Contributions (www.contributionsmagazine.com). The how-to magazine for those working at America's charitable organizations,

Contributions focuses on all facets of fundraising and organizational management. Each issue offers executive directors and development officers a wealth of articles, information, and tips on such subjects as board development, major gifts fundraising, prospect and donor research, direct-mail fundraising, volunteer management, non-profit marketing, Internet and email fundraising, proposal writing, planned giving, and corporate and foundation fundraising.

Corporate Philanthropist (www.corporatephilanthropy.org /research/best-practices/the-corporate-philanthropist.html). The quarterly publication of the Committee Encouraging Corporate Philanthropy (CECP), each issue of *Corporate Philanthropist* (previously called *New Century Philanthropy*) focuses on a relevant trend or focus area in the field of corporate philanthropy. It includes related best practices and perspectives from industry thought leaders, as well as general CECP news and event information.

Council on Foundations. (www.cof.org). The Council on Foundations publishes a variety of electronic newsletters addressing topics of interest to the grantmaking community:

Philanthropy in the News (www.cof.org/about/newsroom/). National and regional media coverage of philanthropy and the charitable sector delivered every morning by email.

Thought > Action > Impact (www.cofinteract.org/taijournal). Published bimonthly, this thought journal gives voice to some of the most influential leaders from the public, private, and non-profit sectors on timely topics. *TAI* offers grantmakers both philosophical perspectives and practical advice relevant to the philanthropic field.

In addition, the Council on Foundations publishes *Our Philanthropy,* a monthly e-newsletter with news, articles, and events of interest to the various kinds of foundations, in four versions:

- Community (www.cof.org/whoweserve/community)
- Corporate (www.cof.org/whoweserve/corporate)
- Family (www.cof.org/whoweserve/family)
- Independent (www.cof.org/whoweserve/privateindependent)

Effect (www.efc.be/NewsKnowledge/Pages/Publications-Effect Magazine.aspx). *Effect* is the European Foundation Centre's flagship publication about and for European foundations, with an emphasis on the Centre's members. The magazine, published twice per year, covers foundations' impact and role in Europe and the world; operational issues; the political, legal, and fiscal environments in which foundations work; and how they get that work done, both individually and in collaboration with others.

FundRaising Success (www.fundraisingsuccessmag.com/). *Fund Raising Success,* founded in 2003, is a practical guide for nonprofit organizations. It exists to provide nonprofits with the most useful and pertinent information, strategies, and expert advice to help them generate the necessary fundraising revenue to fulfill their mission. Encyclopedic in its approach, it covers everything from e-philanthropy and direct mail to donor retention and regulatory issues.

Grantsmanship Center Magazine. Grantsmanship Center publications contain information on how to plan, manage, staff, and fund the programs of nonprofit organizations and government agencies. The *Grantsmanship Center News,* also called *Grantsmanship Center Magazine,* reached over two hundred thousand nonprofit and government agencies at its peak. Although no longer in print, this publication continues to provide a superb historical framework for nonprofit management. Archives are available at the Library of Congress or online at www.tgci.com/magazine.shtml. The Grantsmanship Center currently publishes *Centered,* a monthly digest of useful articles for grantseekers and proposal writers, as well as expert advice from the Grantsmanship Center's trainers. *Centered* delivers practical information that helps sharpen grant research, proposal-writing, evaluation, and team-building skills.

Grassroots Fundraising Journal (www.grassrootsfundraising .org). Published bimonthly by the Grassroots Institute for Fundraising Training, a multiracial organization that promotes the connection between fundraising, social justice, and movement building. This journal was cofounded in 1981 by Kim Klein and Lisa Honig, who saw that most of the resources on nonprofit fundraising are not applicable to grassroots groups, especially those challenging and changing the status quo. The journal provides grassroots organizations with affordable and practical information and ideas for fundraising.

Inspire Your World (www.inspireyourworld.com). The first consumer magazine dedicated to volunteerism, bringing together community leaders, celebrities, CEOs, and everyday people who share a common commitment to giving back. *Inspire Your World* serves as a primary source for news on the nonprofit industry and on companies and individuals dedicated to volunteerism, philanthropy, and community service. Its mission is to generate pathways to action that increase volunteerism and giving by illustrating how companies, nonprofit organizations, and individuals work together to meet the needs of the communities they serve.

Journal for Nonprofit Management (www.supportcenteronline .org/resources.php). This journal, published by the Support Center for Nonprofit Management, is an annual publication for those concerned with developing excellence in nonprofit management. It is a source of thinking and articles on the issues challenging nonprofit organizations today.

Nonprofit and Voluntary Sector Quarterly (http://nvs.sagepub .com/). *Nonprofit and Voluntary Sector Quarterly,* the journal of the Association for Research on Nonprofit Organizations and Voluntary Action, is dedicated to enhancing our knowledge of nonprofit organizations, philanthropy, and voluntarism by providing cutting-edge research, discussion, and analysis of the field, and leads its readers to understand the impact the nonprofit sector has on society. It provides a forum for researchers from around the world to publish timely articles from a variety of disciplinary perspectives.

Nonprofit Board Report (www.pbpinfo.com/nbrpub/default .html). A newsletter offering short articles to help nonprofit executives and boards work together more effectively, tackling issues that nonprofit organizations regularly struggle with. The newsletter offers strategies for fundraising, recruiting board members, helping board members understand their roles, and solving management and financial planning problems.

Nonprofit Quarterly (www.nonprofitquarterly.org). A national journal whose overarching editorial goal is to strengthen the role of nonprofit organizations to activate democracy. The journal is committed to providing a forum for the critical thinking and exploration needed to help nonprofits stay true to this democratic calling and to achieve their potential as effective, powerful, and influential organizations in concert with their constituencies.

The Nonprofit Times (www.nptimes.com). Published twice a month, this publication provides useful information on the business of managing nonprofit organizations, addressing matters pertaining to all aspects of nonprofit management, such as fundraising, financial management, direct marketing, technology, legal issues, and human resources. Free subscriptions are offered to full-time U.S. nonprofit executives.

Nonprofit World (www.snpo.org/publications/nonprofitworld .php). A bimonthly magazine published since 1983 that provides nonprofit leaders with concise and practical articles whose advice can be easily implemented. *Nonprofit World* is published by the Society for Nonprofit Organizations, which provides nonprofit staff members, volunteers, and board members with resources and information to work more effectively and efficiently toward accomplishing their mission.

onPhilanthropy (http://onphilanthropy.com/). Published by CauseWired Communications, *onPhilanthropy* is the leading global e-newsletter for nonprofit, philanthropy, and corporate social engagement professionals. *onPhilanthropy* publishes articles pertaining to the issues that matter most to today's philanthropic community, as well as best practices in the sector.

The Philanthropist (www.thephilanthropist.ca/). A quarterly journal for managers, directors, and legal and financial advisers of Canadian charitable organizations and foundations. It publishes articles and information relevant to the Canadian philanthropic sector and provides a forum for discussion of issues arising in this sector.

Philanthropy (http://philanthropyroundtable.org/). Published by the Philanthropy Roundtable, this bimonthly publication offers coverage and commentary on issues of concern to donors, featuring interviews with philanthropists and advice on foundation management. *Philanthropy* includes coverage of past and ongoing philanthropic efforts and strategies, as well as news stories and commentary relevant to those who are active in the philanthropic sector.

Philanthropy Matters (www.philanthropy.iupui.edu /philanthropymatters/). A semiannual magazine that provides professionals and volunteers with quick and easy access to ideas and news. Each issue contains practical, need-to-know results from the latest research conducted by faculty and staff at the Center on Philanthropy at Indiana University and by other practitioners and scholars around the world.

Philanthropy News Digest (http://foundationcenter.org/pnd/). The *Digest,* a daily news service of the Foundation Center, is a compendium, in digest form, of philanthropy-related articles and features culled from print and electronic media outlets nationwide. Each abstract includes a citation of the original news source, which readers of the *Digest* can use to read the original Web site or to find a copy of the original article.

Philanthropy World (www.philanthropyworld.com/pw-magazine). Celebrates the philanthropic spirit in the United States and around the globe. Published six times a year, *Philanthropy World* features articles on extraordinary people who are dedicated to charitable causes. In addition, each issue highlights areas of philanthropic giving, such as corporate giving, foundations, and volunteering, as well as key nonprofit agencies and contributors. The magazine publishes information that keeps readers up-to-date on the latest important philanthropic happenings around the country and the rest of the world.

Responsive Philanthropy (www.ncrp.org/publications). Published quarterly by the National Committee for Responsive Philanthropy,

Responsive Philanthropy provides comprehensive coverage of trends and critical issues surrounding foundation, corporate, and workplace philanthropy as they affect social justice and the public interest.

Stanford Social Innovation Review (www.ssireview.org). Published quarterly by the Stanford Graduate School of Business, the *Review*'s mission is to share substantive insights and practical experiences that will help those who do the work of improving society do it even better. The main audience is nonprofit executives, grantmaking executives, social entrepreneurs, and corporate executives concerned with social, environmental, and community issues. The *Review* aims to foster an exchange of views among the public, nonprofit, and private sectors, focusing on advancing strategic management and leadership in the social sector.

Trust and Foundation News (www.acf.org.uk/publications andresources/). The Association of Charitable Foundations' quarterly magazine is packed with news, views, and information and provides up-to-date briefings on issues in grantmaking in the United Kingdom.

Voluntas (www.istr.org/?page=VOLUNTAS). *Voluntas* is an interdisciplinary academic journal that publishes articles presenting theoretical and empirical work, introducing new topics and reviews, as well as offering critical commentary on research and policy in the fields of civil society, philanthropy, and the nonprofit sector. *Voluntas* is published by the International Society for Third-Sector Research, a major international association that promotes the creation, discussion, and advancement of knowledge pertaining to the third sector and its impact on human and planetary well-being and development internationally.

Worth (www.worth.com). Aimed at high-net-worth individuals and their advisers, *Worth* reports on issues related to comprehensive wealth management, including investment opportunities, private banking and financial advisory services, business ownership and succession planning, as well as philanthropy, lifestyle, and passion investing.

Who Teaches About the Nonprofit Sector—Academic Programs

Columbia University Business School, Institute for Not-for-Profit Management (www4.gsb.columbia.edu/execed/social-enterprise). For over thirty years, the Institute for Not-for-Profit Management at Executive Education at Columbia Business School has equipped nonprofit and public-sector organizations to be ready to meet the challenges of today's fast-paced and dynamic environments. Through intensive graduate-level programs, participants study core management disciplines tailored to the nonprofit sector. Students in this program learn to develop and use scarce resources, manage growth and competition, and serve their constituents.

Harvard University, Hauser Center for Nonprofit Organizations, John F. Kennedy School of Government (www.hks.harvard.edu/hauser). The Hauser Center seeks to expand understanding of and accelerate critical thinking about civil society among scholars, practitioners, policymakers, and the general public by encouraging scholarship, developing curriculum, fostering mutual learning between academics and practitioners, and shaping policies that enhance the sector and its role in society. It strives to explore the critical questions affecting nonprofits, support teaching about nonprofit organizations across Harvard University, develop curricula in the field, and connect current and future leaders with new thinking and scholarship.

Indiana University Bloomington, School of Public and Environmental Affairs (www.indiana.edu/~spea/). The School of Public and Environmental Affairs (SPEA) at Indiana University is committed to teaching, research, and service in such areas as public and nonprofit management, public policy, environmental science, criminal justice, arts management, and health administration. The school maintains continuing relationships with a large number of public agencies at all levels of government, public and private hospitals and health organizations, nonprofit organizations, and corporations in the private sector. SPEA has earned national distinction for innovative educational programs that combine administrative, social, economic, financial, and science disciplines.

Indiana University, Center on Philanthropy (www.philanthropy .iupui.edu). The Center on Philanthropy pioneered philanthropic studies as an academic subject, exploring and explaining both the theory and practice of how and why philanthropy works. Offering master's and doctoral degrees in philanthropic studies as well as lifelong learning opportunities, the Center applies a liberal arts approach that studies and teaches the subject from a variety of disciplines using qualitative and quantitative approaches. The Center is a leading academic center dedicated to increasing the understanding of philanthropy, improving its practice, and enhancing participation in philanthropy through research, teaching, public service, and public affairs programs in philanthropy, fundraising, and management of nonprofit organizations.

Johns Hopkins University Center for Civil Society Studies, Institute for Policy Studies (www.jhu.edu/~ccss/). The Center for Civil Society Studies seeks to improve understanding and the effective functioning of nonprofit, philanthropic, and civil society organizations in the United States and throughout the rest of the world in order to enhance the contribution these organizations can make to democracy and the quality of human life. The center is part of the Johns Hopkins Institute for Policy Studies and carries out its work through a combination of research, training, and information sharing both domestically and internationally. The institute features a distinguished staff of policy professionals covering economic development, housing and urban policy, human resource development policy, and many other major social issues.

The Maxwell School of Syracuse University, Campbell Public Affairs Institute (www.maxwell.syr.edu/). The Nonprofit Studies Program was established under the auspices of the Campbell Public Affairs Institute to create and facilitate sharing of knowledge about nonprofit governance, management, and policy. Its mission is to examine the ideal of citizenship, its evolution, and the conditions under which it thrives. The program ties together nonprofit research, outreach, and teaching activities to explore the relationship among citizens, private organizations, and government in an effort to improve understanding of the development and implementation of effective leadership, management, and policy.

New York University, Heyman Center for Philanthropy and Fundraising, School of Continuing & Professional Studies (www.scps.nyu.edu/areas-of-study/philanthropy-fundraising/). The Heyman Center is one of the preeminent educators of fundraisers and grantmakers, offering a solid foundation in the field while helping students develop their own fundraising philosophy and framework through advanced study of the history and theory of the industry. Heyman Center offerings include graduate-level and certificate coursework in grantmaking, foundations, fundraising, and global philanthropy geared toward practitioners, executives, and volunteers from nonprofits, corporations, and foundations.

New York University, Robert F. Wagner Graduate School of Public Service (http://wagner.nyu.edu). Established in 1938, the Robert F. Wagner Graduate School of Public Service offers advanced programs that educate future leaders of public, nonprofit, and health institutions as well as private organizations serving the public sector. Trained in management, policy, and finance, Wagner students graduate with the skills they need to confront society's most pressing problems. NYU Wagner offers a dynamic approach to preparing people to serve the public through education, research, and service. It delivers a practical approach with an urban focus and global perspective.

Northwestern University Kellogg School of Management, Center for Nonprofit Management (www.kellogg.northwestern.edu/research/nonprofit/index.htm). Founded in 1998, the Center's mission is to become an internationally recognized resource in the field of nonprofit management education and higher education through graduate-degree and executive-management programs. The Center aims to harness the resources of the Kellogg School of Management at Northwestern University to partner with the nonprofit community. It relies on both academic faculty and practitioners from various areas of the nonprofit sector to form a bridge between the academic community and the nonprofit sector.

Stanford University Graduate School of Business, Center for Social Innovation (www.gsb.stanford.edu/csi). The Graduate School of Business believes that business schools have a responsibility to teach students to be innovative, principled, and insightful leaders who can change the world. The Center represents a cornerstone of the school's multidisciplinary approach to management and leadership education. It invests its resources in an integrated set of activities that are designed to enhance the leadership and management capacity of individuals who strive to create social and environmental value. Through the discovery and worldwide dissemination of new ideas, the Center increases awareness of social problems and provides frameworks for thinking about and solving these problems.

UCLA Center for Civil Society (www.spa.ucla.edu/ccs). The Center for Civil Society is the focal point for UCLA's School of Public Affairs programs in nonprofit leadership and management, grassroots advocacy, nongovernmental organizations, and philanthropy. It coordinates teaching on nonprofit organizations and aspects of civil society; conducts research; and offers seminars, conferences, colloquia, and executive education as part of community engagement. In undertaking these mutually supporting activities, it seeks to contribute to the policy dialogue on the current and future role of nonprofit organizations, philanthropy, and civil society.

University of California, Berkeley, Haas School of Business, Center for Nonprofit and Public Leadership (http://nonprofit .haas.berkeley.edu/). The Center prepares leaders with practical business skills to found, lead, manage, and govern nonprofit and public organizations for the public good. It provides MBA students an opportunity to augment the core business curriculum with specialized coursework, practical application, and career opportunities in public and nonprofit management.

University of Minnesota, Humphrey Institute of Public Affairs (www.hhh.umn.edu). The Humphrey Institute is widely recognized for its role in examining public issues and shaping public policy at the local, state, national, and international levels, and for providing leadership and management expertise to public and nonprofit organizations. The institute uses its resources and those of the university to prepare students for leadership in public affairs, bridge disciplines across the university and larger community to advance public affairs scholarship, and encourage public engagement and scholarship to address important issues facing Minnesota, the nation, and the world in a nonpartisan setting.

University of Southern California School of Policy, Planning and Development, Center on Philanthropy and Public Policy (www.usc.edu/schools/sppd/philanthropy). The Center on Philanthropy and Public Policy acts as a catalyst for understanding and action at the intersection of the public, private, and nonprofit sectors by providing information and analysis of value to decision makers in the three sectors. The master of public administration program reflects both the breadth and diversity of the ever-changing nature of public administration. Through research and communications, the Center provides information about the changing philanthropic landscape, profiles the resulting challenges for the sector and for society, and stimulates conversation to foster understanding and to advance public problem solving.

University of Utah, Center for Public Policy and Administration (www.cppa.utah.edu/). The University of Utah MPA program, established in 1976, has built a strong local, regional, and national reputation, producing alumni in all fields of public and nonprofit administration. The university administers the MPA program through the independent Center for Public Policy and Administration, thereby offering an opportunity to develop a multidisciplinary program, but having primary affiliations with the Department of Political Science. From its inception, the program has been rigorous, requiring integrative core and elective coursework, practical administrative experience, and a major research paper. Over the past thirty years, the program has been revised and updated regularly to respond to the changing environment, including the growth of the nonprofit sector.

University of Washington, Evans School of Public Affairs (http://evans.washington.edu). The Evans School was founded in 1962 as the nation's first school of public affairs at a public university. Evans draws on its partnerships with public, nonprofit, and private organizations to work across political lines to promote civil civic dialogue in service of the public interest. Public Service Clinics enable students and faculty to partner with organizations to design policies and institutions that lead to more livable communities, improve human services, and protect our natural resources. The Civic Engagement for the 21st Century project cultivates broad and effective participation in solving complex community challenges, including housing, transportation, education, and growth management. Faculty, students, and staff serve on boards and committees and as consultants for numerous local, national, and global organizations.

RESOURCE B

Major Supporters of Capacity Building

ACCORDING TO THE FOUNDATION CENTER'S ONLINE directory and the Philanthropic Capacity Building Resources database, the following foundations have expressed an interest in capacity building as a grantmaking priority:

The Arca Foundation, Washington, DC (www.arcafoundation.org)

Bruner Foundation, Inc., Cambridge, MA (www.brunerfoundation .org)

The Annie E. Casey Foundation, Baltimore, MD (www.aecf.org)

The O. P. and W. E. Edwards Foundation, Inc., Red Lodge, MT (http://opweedwards.org)

Firelight Foundation, Santa Cruz, CA (www.firelightfoundation .org)

The Ford Foundation, New York, NY (www.fordfoundation.org)

Evelyn and Walter Haas Jr. Fund, San Francisco, CA (www .haasjr.org)

Ewing Marion Kauffman Foundation, Kansas City, MO (www .kauffman.org)

John S. and James L. Knight Foundation, Miami, FL (www .knightfoundation.org)

Lilly Endowment Inc., Indianapolis, IN (www.lillyendowment .org)

The John D. and Catherine T. MacArthur Foundation, Chicago, IL (www.macfound.org)

Charles Stewart Mott Foundation, Flint, MI (www.mott.org)

William J. and Dorothy K. O'Neill Foundation, Inc., Cleveland, OH (www.oneillfdn.org)

The Oak Foundation U.S.A., Portland, ME (www.oakfnd.org)

The David and Lucile Packard Foundation, Los Altos, CA (www.packard.org)

RGK Foundation, Austin, TX (www.rgkfoundation.org)

May and Stanley Smith Charitable Trust, Sausalito, CA (www .adminitrustllc.com/may-and-stanley-smith-charitable-trust/)

Surdna Foundation, Inc., New York, NY (www.surdna.org)

The Wallace Foundation, New York, NY (www.wallacefoundation .org)

NOTES

Chapter 1

1. Jewish World Watch. *Solar Cooker Project Evaluation: Iridimi Refugee Camp, Chad.* Retrieved from www.jewishworldwatch.org/wp-content/uploads/2010/06/Solar_Cooker_Project_Evaluation.pdf, October 2007, p. 12.

Chapter 4

1. Wolf, T. *Managing a Nonprofit Organization in the Twenty-First Century.* (Rev. and updated ed.) New York: Fireside, 1999, p. 286.

Chapter 7

1. Power, S. *A Problem from Hell: America and the Age of Genocide.* New York: Basic Books, 2002, p. xviii.

Chapter 8

1. Harlem Children's Zone. *Growth Plan FY2001–FY2009.* Retrieved from www.hcz.org/images/stories/pdfs/business_plan.pdf, p. 30.
2. Harlem Children's Zone. *Consolidated Financial Statements Together with Report of Independent Certified Public Accountants: Harlem Children's Zone and Affiliate: As of June 30, 2010.* Retrieved from www.hcz.org/images /stories/pdfs/HCZ_2010_Basic_Financial_Statements.pdf, p. 3.
3. Ibid., p. 12.
4. Project HEALTH. "Project HEALTH: Breaking the Link Between Poverty and Poor Health" [fact sheet]. Retrieved from www.jhsph.edu/source /VolunteerAgencies/AdvocacyOrgs/ProjHlthfactsheet.pdf.

Chapter 16

1. VisionSpring. *VisionSpring Annual Report: 2010*. Retrieved from www
   .guidestar.org/ViewEdoc.aspx?eDocId=520649&approved=True.
2. Giving USA Foundation. *Giving USA 2011: The Annual Report on Phi-lanthropy for the Year 2010*. Chicago: Giving USA Foundation, 2011,
   p. 4.

ACKNOWLEDGMENTS

LITTLE DID WE KNOW THAT we would have the energy and temerity to develop a second work on the heels of *The Art of Giving: Where the Soul Meets a Business Plan*. We were driven by two important motives. One was to write a book that would engage the very many philanthropists with limited financial resources who passionately desire to change the world. The living examples in this book will, we hope, show that indeed this can be and is being done!

The second motive was more selfish. We so enjoyed writing *The Art of Giving,* we thought we could replicate that experience. It was also a great pleasure to meet with so many people as a result of that work; individuals who made us feel like we had, indeed, created leverage by writing of our experiences and approaches to philanthropy.

Once again, we are grateful to our partner and collaborator, the writer John Sedgwick, who continues to shape our thoughts in language that is incredibly accessible. We are very fortunate to have collaborated with him and befriended him. Our colleagues at the Andrea and Charles Bronfman Philanthropies continue to provide us with the support that allowed this work to be done. We especially acknowledge Sharna Goldseker and Janet Aviad. We are particularly grateful to Jill Collier-Indyk, executive director of the Charles Bronfman Prize Foundation, who identified many of the humanitarians we highlight throughout this work. Yvonne Deery has done it again. Her research, fact checking, and continuous effort to make sure we get it right is invaluable. John Hoover, our intrepid chief financial officer, again made sure that we have the right perspective. Our long-standing assistants Angela Forster and Barbara Plotnick continue to show amazingly good cheer as we complicate their lives with endless projects. Our heartfelt thanks to them both.

We were pleased to have had the opportunity to again work with the extraordinary staff at Jossey-Bass, an imprint of Wiley. Our editor, Karen Murphy, made us stay more focused for a clearer work. All of her good-natured colleagues, especially Robin Lloyd, Meredith Stanton, Alina Poniewaz, Adrian Morgan, Teresa Hennessy, John Maas, Michele Jones, and Cedric Crocker, have really gone above and beyond to produce this work in a superb and timely fashion. We are also grateful to our agents, Kate Lee and Andrea Barzvi, and their team at ICM, who once again guided us so very well. Jeff's wife, Audrey Weiner, who is also completing her second book, found the time and good cheer to make this work seem important. Finally, we acknowledge the eighteen nonprofit social entrepreneurs who inspired the stories and the lessons in this work, along with those whom we didn't have a chance to highlight who are impassioned and continuously create programs and projects that improve the world.

ABOUT THE AUTHORS

CHARLES BRONFMAN IS CHAIRMAN of the Andrea and Charles Bronfman Philanthropies, which he created with his late wife in 1985. He has had several careers, many at the same time. He joined the Seagram Company in 1952, a business founded by his father, Samuel Bronfman. He began as a trainee and moved up through the ranks, holding such titles as president of the Canadian Subsidiaries and liaison officer to the DuPont Company. Shortly after the formation of Vivendi Universal in December 2000 and coinciding with his fiftieth anniversary of employment at Seagram, Bronfman, then cochairman of the company, retired from the business. In 1968 he became the principal owner of the Montreal Expos, a position he held until 1991, when the club was sold. It was the first major league baseball team to exist outside the United States.

Bronfman began his philanthropic career at the age of seventeen. He was president of the Montreal Federation from 1973 to 1974. He joined the board of the Center for Learning and Leadership in 1992 and was its chair from 1998 until he was named founding chair of the United Jewish Communities in 1999, a post he held until 2001. He currently sits on the boards of trustees of Mount Sinai Medical Center (New York City) and Harlem Village Academies (New York City) and is a member of the International Council of Hillel. Included in his honors was making the first ceremonial pitch at the World Series in Toronto in 1992, the first such contest ever to be played outside the United States. He became a member of the Queen's Privy Council for Canada and a Companion of the Order of Canada, the highest civilian honor in that country. He, with his late wife, Andrea, was awarded honorary citizenship of Jerusalem. Bronfman holds honorary degrees from six universities located in Canada, the United States, and Israel.

JEFFREY SOLOMON IS THE PRESIDENT of the Andrea and Charles Bronfman Philanthropies, a group of foundations operating in Canada, Israel, and the United States. Among the foundation's innovative launches are Birthright Israel, a program bringing hundreds of thousands of young adults to Israel for a ten-day trip; the Gift of New York, a powerful response to the terrorist attacks of September 11, 2001, helping ease the suffering of the families of victims through the healing power of culture; and Project Involvement, an educational reform program serving some 265,000 Israeli elementary school students.

Solomon has also served as senior vice president and chief operating officer of UJA-Federation of New York, president of AltroHealth and Rehabilitation Services in New York, and associate executive director of both the Miami Jewish Home and Hospital for the Aged and Miami Jewish Family and Children's Services. Solomon also served with the New York City and New York State governments, as well as with the federal government in Washington DC and its regional offices in New York and Atlanta. An author of over eighty publications, he has been an adjunct associate professor at New York University and a lecturer at the University of Miami Department of Architecture and Columbia University School of Business. He has had academic clinical appointments from six universities in four states. He has served on numerous nonprofit and foundation boards, including the FJC, a community foundation in New York; and the Council on Foundations, where he chaired the Committee on Ethics and Practice and served on its executive committee. He is a founding trustee of the World Faiths Development Dialogue and has received a number of honors from professional associations and universities.

INDEX

271

Index